STUDIES IN EUSEBIUS

STUDIES IN EUSEBIUS

BY

J. STEVENSON

Sometime Scholar and Naden Divinity Student of
St John's College, Cambridge, and Visiting
Fellow in Princeton University

Thirlwall Prize Essay
1927

CAMBRIDGE
AT THE UNIVERSITY PRESS
MCMXXIX

CAMBRIDGE
UNIVERSITY PRESS

University Printing House, Cambridge CB2 8BS, United Kingdom

Published in the United States of America by Cambridge University Press, New York

Cambridge University Press is part of the University of Cambridge.

It furthers the University's mission by disseminating knowledge in the pursuit of education, learning and research at the highest international levels of excellence.

www.cambridge.org
Information on this title: www.cambridge.org/9781107426702

© Cambridge University Press 1929

First published 1929
First paperback edition 2014

A catalogue record for this publication is available from the British Library

ISBN 978-1-107-42670-2 Paperback

PREFACE

Ἀλλά μοι συγγνώμην εὐγνωμόνων ἐντεῦθεν ὁ λόγος αἰτεῖ,
μείζονα ἢ καθ' ἡμετέραν δύναμιν ὁμολογῶν εἶναι τὴν ἐπαγγελίαν
ἐντελῆ καὶ ἀπαράλειπτον ὑποσχεῖν (Eus. *H.E.* I. I. 3).

Thus did Eusebius crave indulgence at the beginning of his *Church History*, and I cannot find a
better quotation with which to preface this work,
which is neither 'complete' nor 'perfect'. It does
not cover the whole of the life and works of
Eusebius, and has no pretensions to being the last
word even on the topics with which it deals. The
literature bearing on the period covered by the
life of Eusebius is enormous, and in the case of one
who has been unable to give a lifetime to studying
it, a great deal of this literature has of necessity
been neglected. Originally this work was planned
on a much more ambitious scale, but as pressure
of teaching duties made it impossible to see when it
could be completed, I decided to publish it more
or less in the form in which it was awarded a
Thirlwall Medal in 1927. It may be pointed out
that the work, in its present form, deals with
two distinct periods in the life of Eusebius. After
the introductory chapter, it deals with his life to
the end of the Great Persecution (chaps. II and III),

and then with his position in the Arian controversy (chaps. iv–vi).

I wish to thank many friends for assistance given at various times; in particular, I wish to thank Mr T. R. Glover, at whose suggestion I first began to work on Eusebius, for constant encouragement, Mr Norman H. Baynes, for help and advice on many occasions, and for bringing to my notice works of which I should not otherwise have known, and Professor N. H. Parker, my colleague in Toronto from 1925 to 1928, for reading my manuscript and pointing out various matters of detail. Finally, I wish to thank the Syndics of the University Press for undertaking the publication of the work, and the Press reader for saving me from many pitfalls.

J. STEVENSON

UNIVERSITY COLLEGE OF SWANSEA
Advent 1928

CONTENTS

CHAPTER I

The City and Church of Caesarea

Strabo the geographer makes but a brief reference[1] to Strato's Tower. In his course southwards along the Syrian coast he merely mentions it, and the fact that there was a landing-place there. But even as Strabo wrote, or perhaps before he had written, a transformation was taking place, and the munificence of a king was changing this decaying[2] spot into a splendid city, and the only real port in Palestine.

Strato's Tower was not a place of great antiquity, as its neighbours to the north and south, Dora and Joppa, were. It is probable that the founder of the town was one of the two Stratos who were Kings of Sidon in the fourth century B.C. We do not know anything about its early history; in Josephus it first emerges in the story of the murder of Antigonus by his brother Aristobulus.[3] It had been prophesied of Antigonus, as of Cambyses, Epaminondas, King Henry the Fourth of

[1] P. 758. On Strato's Tower and Caesarea see L. Haefeli, *Cäsarea am Meer* (Münster i. W. 1923).
[2] Jos. *B.J.* I. 21. 5 (408). Had Strato's Tower been destroyed in the earthquake of 31 B.C.?
[3] After 104 B.C. and before 102–1 (fall of Cleopatra). Bevan, *House of Seleucus*, II. 256–7. Jos. *A.J.* XIII. 11. 12 (307 ff.).

SE   I   I

England and others, that he should die at a certain place, in his case Strato's Tower. But Antigonus was murdered in Jerusalem, and the prophet thought that he had lost his reputation, till it was discovered that the murder had been committed in a tower of the same name as the city on the coast. At this time one Zoilus was tyrant of Strato's Tower and of its neighbour Dora, but he was overcome by Ptolemy Lathyrus at the request of Alexander Jannaeus,[1] and his dominion passed to the Jews. One can infer that the inhabitants were compelled to adopt Jewish customs.[2]

With the coming of Pompey to Palestine in 63 B.C. the coast cities, Gaza, Joppa, Dora, and Strato's Tower, as well as various inland towns, were added[3] to the province of Syria, and Strato's Tower must have been one of the places bequeathed by Antony to Cleopatra.[4] At the final triumph of Augustus, Herod received various towns, including Strato's Tower, as an addition to his dominions, in recompense for his friendship, of which[5] he took good care that Augustus should not be ignorant. Herod built himself a new capital, Sebaste, on the site of the ancient Samaria, but more than a new capital was needed: an ambitious

---

[1] *A.J.* xiii. 12. 4 (335).   [2] *A.J.* xiii. 15. 4 (397).
[3] *A.J.* xiv. 4. 4 (76). *B.J.* i. 7. 7 (156).
[4] *A.J.* xv. 4. 1 (95).   [5] Cf. *A.J.* xv. 7. 3 (217).

monarch required a port as well, and of the coast towns he chose Strato's Tower as a fit subject for his munificence. The coast[1] was harbourless; ships had to ride at anchor off the shore, as the prevalent south winds drove the waves against the rocks with such fury that the backward surge disturbed the sea for a considerable distance, or by rolling to the shore sand from the sea created sandbanks.[2] Nevertheless, Strato's Tower seems to have been a stopping-place much used on the voyage from Phoenicia to Egypt.[3] Herod determined to build a port at this place. But he did not have it all his own way; in his building he had a formidable contest with the forces of nature: all the material had to be brought[4] from elsewhere, and the struggle to combine beauty and utility was hard, but the king won, and the city of Caesarea was built, in construction a compliment to the tenacity of Herod, and in name a compliment to his imperial benefactor. Herod really had an eye on Rome when he built Caesarea. Josephus states that this city was an especial demonstration of the king's love of magnificence.[5] It was also a strong

[1] Cf. *A.J.* xv. 9. 6 (333) with *B.J.* I. 21. 5 (409).

[2] I think that this is what Josephus means in *A.J. loc. cit.* There is a reference in the Talmud to the sand at Caesarea. Haefeli, *op. cit.* p. 12.

[3] *A.J. loc. cit.*

[4] *A.J.* xv. 9. 6 (332).

[5] *B.J.* I. 2. I (410).

1-2

fortress for his personal safety.[1] Well did Herod know the passionate, easily excited character of the Jews.[2]

The new city was on a plain by the sea shore,[3] stifling in summer and warm in winter. Vespasian recognised it as a good place to winter in during the Jewish war.[4] Later accounts agree that Caesarea was in a pleasant land; the Talmud calls the towns of Tyre and Caesarea 'the country of life',[5] and the geographer Mukaddasi[6] says, 'There is no city more beautiful nor any better filled with good things; plenty has its well spring here, and useful products are on every hand'.

Herod had a magnificent harbour built. So famous did this harbour become that the city was designated by it.[7] Josephus says in one[8] passage that it was as big as the Peiraeus, in another[9] that it was bigger. The breakwater enclosing the harbour was made by dropping huge stones into the sea and was 200 feet broad. On it was a sea wall, lodgings for the sailors, and before these a

[1] *A.J.* xv. 8. 5 (293, 295).   [2] Haefeli, *op. cit.* p. 11.
[3] *B.J.* III. 9. 1 (413).   [4] *B.J.* IV. 2. 1 (87).
[5] A. Neubauer, *Géographie du Talmud*, p. 13.
[6] Transl. in *Palestine under the Moslems* by G. le Strange, p. 474.
[7] Καισάρεια ἡ πρὸς Σεβαστῷ λιμένι. Pauly-Wissowa, *Real-enzyklopädie der klassischen Altertumswissenschaft*, art. 'Caesarea', col. 1292.   [8] *A.J.* xv. 9. 6 (332).
[9] *B.J.* I. 21. 5 (410). Both the statements of Josephus are exaggerations. Haefeli, *op. cit.* p. 14.

4

'most pleasant'[1] walk round the whole length of
the structure. At intervals towers were set, and
of these Josephus singles out the tower of Drusus
for special[2] mention. The entrance to the harbour,
with a great monument on either side, faced the
north,[3] the most sheltered direction. Opposite to
this entrance, on rising ground, was the temple of
Caesar and Rome wherein, in imitation of the
statue of Zeus at Olympia, and that of Hera at
Argos, the two divinities had their abode.

The other public buildings, amphitheatre,
theatre and agora, were on an equally lavish scale,
all the city being built[4] of white stone. In the
192nd Olympiad (12–8 B.C.), in the twenty-eighth
year of Herod's reign (10–9 B.C.), the first celebration of Games, named like the city from Caesar,
took place, this festival marking the completion of
the new city,[5] after ten or twelve years' building.
But the old name of the city was not entirely
forgotten, and in Ptolemy,[6] in the Clementine

[1] *A.J.* xv. 9. 6 (337).

[2] *A.J. loc. cit.* (336), πάνυ καλόν τι χρῆμα.

[3] Accurately speaking, the harbour mouth faced north-
west. Haefeli, *op. cit.* p. 14.

[4] *A.J.* xvi. 5. 1 (136). *B.J.* I. 21. 8 (415). Cf. *A.J.* xv.
9. 6 (339), Καισάρεια...καλλίστης καὶ τῆς ὕλης καὶ τῆς
κατασκευῆς τετυχηκυῖα.

[5] Cf. *A.J.* xvi. 5. 1 (136) with xv. 9. 6 (341).

[6] Schürer, *History of Jewish People in the time of Jesus Christ*,
Eng. transl. div. II, vol. I, p. 85. This name appears in the
Armenian translation of the *Chronicle* of Eusebius also,

5

Homilies and *Recognitions*, and in Epiphanius, we find a combination of the two, Caesarea of Strato.

The previous lack of a port on the coast of Palestine, the residence of the Roman governor in the city after the deposition of Archelaus, Herod's successor, and the establishing of a Roman garrison maintained the importance of Caesarea in the future.

From A.D. 41 to 44 the city was under the rule of Herod Agrippa I, who was a benefactor of the Jews. On the occasion of a great festival at Caesarea, in his pride he did not rebuke the flattery of the people, who hailed him as a god, and he was straightway punished by the sudden attack of a fell disease. There are two accounts of his death; one in Josephus,[1] and one in the Acts of the Apostles;[2] both bear witness to the sudden intervention of Heaven, and a unification of the two was attempted by some Christian, who turned an owl[3] into an angel, who appeared as the minister of Heaven's vengeance on the proud ruler. The people of Caesarea vilified the memory of Herod[4] Agrippa, whom they really hated for his Judaising

Schoene, *Eusebii Chronicorum libri duo*, vol. II, p. 152; and it is found in an inscription of the time of Marcus Aurelius at Aphrodisias in Caria and (in Latin) on a military diploma of Vespasian (Haefeli, *op. cit.* p. 26).

[1] *A.J.* XIX. 8. 2 (343 ff.).
[2] Acts xii. 20 ff.   [3] Eus. *H.E.* II. 10.
[4] *Jewish Encyclopedia*, vol. III, p. 488, art. 'Caesarea'.

tendencies, and their behaviour was so bad[1] as to provoke the resentment of the Emperor himself. The city was always Gentile rather than Jewish.[2] That it was never meant to be a Jewish city is shown by the prominence given by its founder to such Gentile buildings as the amphitheatre and the temple of Caesar and Rome. Josephus[3] calls it 'Caesarea, the biggest city of Judaea, inhabited by Greeks for the most part'. This Gentile preponderance was, no doubt, accentuated by the massacre of the Caesarean Jews—20,000 of them, if we may believe Josephus—at the outbreak of the Jewish war, and by the plantation of a colony there by Vespasian, after the war was over.[4]

But previous to the Jewish war the Jews were a formidable minority[5] and the struggle between them and the Gentiles became serious in the reign of Nero, when Felix was governor. The cause lay in the fact that each side denied ἰσοπολίτεια to the other: 'for the Jews', says Josephus,[6] 'thought to take the first place because the founder of Caesarea,

---

[1] *A.J.* xix. 9. 2 (361 ff.).

[2] Cf. the Letter of Apollonius of Tyana to the Chie Councillors of Caesarea, in which he commends the ἤθη Ἑλληνικά of the city. Given in Philostratus' *Life of Apollonius*, vol. ii, p. 416 (Loeb Library).

[3] *B.J.* iii. 9. 1 (409).   [4] Pliny, *N.H.* v. 13. 69.

[5] The Jews do not appear to have lived in any particular quarter of the city; cf. *B.J.* ii. 13. 7 (266).

[6] *A.J.* xx. 8. 7 (173 ff.).

7

Herod their king, was a Jew by race, but the Syrians, while agreeing about Herod, said that Caesarea was formerly called Strato's Tower and that at that time they had not a single Jewish inhabitant'. Timely chastisement of the leaders on both sides by the rulers quelled the trouble for a moment, but it began again, the Jews relying on their wealth, the Syrians on the fact that most of the garrison were natives of Caesarea and Sebaste. The custom prevalent in the first century of allowing troops to take root in a place had already become a cause of danger in Caesarea in the reign of Claudius; after the death of Herod Agrippa at Caesarea the gross behaviour of the soldiers had caused Claudius[1] to express the intention of sending them to Pontus; but they begged themselves off, and were, says Josephus, the beginning of the greatest misfortunes to the Jews. Vespasian removed them at last.

Riots took place, and Felix, the governor, called out the troops, who seem to have concentrated their energies on the Jews, and when Felix was succeeded by Festus, these sent to Rome to complain about the acts of Felix,[2] who extricated himself through the influence of Pallas. Moreover Nero, acting on the advice of Beryllus,[3] his secretary for Greek correspondence, who had been bribed

---

[1] *A.J.* xix. 9. 2 (365).   [2] *A.J.* xx. 8. 9 (182–4).
[3] ? Beryllus or Burrhus; cf. Schürer, *op. cit.* div. i, vol. ii, p. 184 note, with P.W. s.v. 'Beryllus'.

by two of the leading Gentiles of Caesarea, decided the question at issue in favour of the Syrians
and matters in Caesarea went from bad to worse.
A Gentile insult to a synagogue[1] produced another
riot, and the Jews retired from the city. Florus,
who was now governor, was quite unsympathetic
to the appeals of the Jews, his sole objects being,
according to the Jewish historian, to get money
out of them, and to cover his own crimes by goading
them to revolt. He compelled the Jews to return
to Caesarea, and there they were massacred,[2] on
the same day as the massacre of the Romans at
Jerusalem. This synchronism need not be pressed;
one cannot be sure if the one massacre was not in
some measure a reprisal for the other. Anyhow,
Caesarea was denuded of its Jewish population, as
Florus took prisoner those who escaped the sword,
and sent them to the dockyards for compulsory
labour.

The war had begun. A Jewish offensive directed
against Caesarea, amongst other places, was un-
successful at this point,[3] and during the war
Caesarea played an important part as a Roman
base. Vespasian[4] landed there after the capture of
Jotopata, and the historian Josephus, as the de-
feated enemy commander, experienced the vocal
resentment of the inhabitants. Vespasian wintered

---

[1] *B.J.* II. 14. 5 (289 ff.).   [2] *B.J.* II. 18. 1 (457 ff.).
[3] *B.J.* II. 18. 1 (459).   [4] *B.J.* III. 9. 1 (409 ff.).

9

two legions there, but forbore to inflict a third upon the city. After the news of the accession of Vitellius to the imperial power it was at Caesarea that the dissatisfaction of the troops of Vespasian with the new sovereign seems to have come to a head,[1] and here it was that the rule of the Empire was first thrust by the Eastern army on its commander. After the fall of Jerusalem Titus celebrated the birthday of his brother at Caesarea with games in which a great multitude of captives were slain.

The plantation of a colony by Vespasian would make up the loss of population occasioned by the war and later in its history the city received another honour from the Emperor of the time, Alexander Severus, who added the title 'Metropolis'.[2] A bare notice in the *Chronicle* of Eusebius states that Nicopolis and Caesarea were destroyed by an earthquake about A.D. 130.[3]

We know little of the history of the city in the second and third centuries. It must have continued a busy place: we hear of purple-dyeing[4] there, and that the land abounded in wine, oil and corn. And the Jews had returned; one reason for this was probably the fact that Jerusalem was forbidden

[1] *B.J.* IV. 10. 4 (601 ff.).

[2] Schürer, *op. cit.* div. II, vol. I, p. 84.

[3] Schoene, *op. cit.* vol. II, p. 166. *Ann. Abr.* 2145. J. Karst, *Die Chronik aus dem Armenischen übersetzt* (p. 220), gives 2144.

[4] Müller, *Geog. Gr. Minor.* vol. II, p. 513 (c. 29), quoted by Schürer, *op. cit.* div. II, vol. I, p. 42.

them after the last siege in Hadrian's reign. We hear[1] of Abbahu, an antagonist of Christianity in the third century, and there are many 'Rabbis of Caesarea'.[2] Nevertheless the Jews hated the city, which they called the 'daughter[3] of Edom' and 'city of abomination and blasphemy'. Very numerous were the deities within its gates: on the coins of Caesarea we find represented Zeus, Poseidon, Apollo, Heracles, Dionysus, Athene, Nike, Serapis and Astarte.[4]

Besides Judaism, there was one other religion which had so far left no impression on the coins of the city. In the history of the earliest Christians no place had played a more important part than Caesarea. Philip, apostle, or evangelist, was the first preacher of the Gospel there,[5] and the evangelist certainly had his home in the city for some time. At Caesarea the Holy Spirit was outpoured on the Gentiles[6]—an event which perhaps changed the course of Christian history. Caesarea was the port used by St Paul,[7] who was tried here also before Felix[8] and Festus and may have written several of his epistles here. A Christian community seems to have existed in the city from the time of the first preaching[9] of the Gospel, but the only name we

[1] *Jewish Enc. loc. cit.*   [2] Neubauer, *op. cit.* pp. 95, 96.
[3] Neubauer, *op. cit.* pp. 91, 96.
[4] List in Schürer, *op. cit.* div. II, vol. I, p. 17.
[5] Acts viii. 40.   [6] Acts x. 44.   [7] Acts xxi. 8.
[8] Acts xxiv–xxv.   [9] Acts xviii. 22, xxi. 16.

possess is that of Cornelius the centurion. The end
of the Acts of the Apostles rings down the curtain
on the Church of Caesarea, as it does on so much
of Christian history. This Church is not mentioned
in any other book of the New Testament; and does
not emerge from complete obscurity till about
A.D. 190. About that time a Synod was held in
Palestine on the Quarto-deciman question,[1] and
Theophilus, Bishop of Caesarea, and Narcissus,
Bishop of Jerusalem, presided over it. With them[2]
were associated Cassius of Tyre and Clarus of
Ptolemais. The end of their synodical letter is
preserved: it shows a great desire that it should be
quite clear that they observed Easter on the same
day as the Church in Alexandria did.

Notwithstanding the lack of positive evidence,
the successive sieges of Jerusalem must have tended
to elevate the Church of Caesarea. After the last
siege of Jerusalem in Hadrian's reign, the old
Jewish Church there, the true mother Church of
Christendom, came to an end, and a Gentile
Church, quite a different organisation altogether,
took its place. The archaeological propensities of
this new congregation eventually made up for its
lack of a pedigree. By the end of the third century
it possessed the authentic bishop's chair of James
the Just, the brother of the Lord; in the early fourth
century the discovery of the Holy Sepulchre and

[1] Eus. *H.E.* v. 23.   [2] Eus. *H.E.* v. 23 and 25.

the Cave of the Resurrection and the influx of pilgrims to visit the city gave it a really eminent position; and finally the Jerusalem Church was made into a fifth Patriarchate at the Council of Chalcedon in A.D. 451.

The earliest notice that we possess about any early Christian relics in Caesarea is in Jerome,[1] who writing at the beginning of the fifth century states that Paula, in her pilgrimage, passed through Caesarea, 'in qua Cornelii domum, Christi vidit ecclesiam, et Philippi aediculas et cubicula quatuor virginum prophetarum'. Thus by the end of the fourth century Caesarea possessed its full complement of memorials; the mention of the house of Cornelius as a church seems to suggest that Cornelius was regarded as the original founder of the Caesarean Church, while the mention of the 'cubicula quatuor' of the daughters of Philip looks like a contribution from fourth-century monasticism to the history of the first century.

From the beginning of the third century onwards, however, the Caesarean Church has a more or less coherent history. It was not really through any merit of its own that it attained to this, but through the arrival of a stranger, Origen, the Christian scholar from Alexandria. His first visit to Caesarea[2] was for safety's sake during a troubled[3] period in

[1] *Ep.* cviii. 8.   [2] Eus. *H.E.* vi. 19.
[3] Caracalla's visit in A.D. 216?.

13

his own city. Alexander of Jerusalem, and Theoctistus of Caesarea, the most illustrious bishops of
Palestine, allowed him—no doubt a tribute to his
reputation—to expound the Scriptures and preach
in church publicly, though he had not been
ordained as presbyter. Demetrius, Bishop of
Alexandria, took this ill, and seems to have pro-
tested to the bishops concerned, who defended
their act by quoting precedents. This shows that
the practice of allowing laymen to preach was not
a universal[1] custom. The controversy died away,
and Demetrius asked Origen to return, which he
did.

About A.D. 231 Origen set out to visit Greece
on ecclesiastical business. On his way he passed
through Caesarea and was ordained presbyter by
the Palestinian bishops, who probably wanted to
hear him preach again, and also wanted to have
no more trouble with the Bishop of Alexandria.
But Demetrius, quite naturally, regarded this act
as a violation of the custom of the Church, and
possibly a slight to himself. A Synod at Alexandria
decided that Origen should leave Alexandria, and
should not reside[2] or teach there. Origen naturally

[1] McGiffert, Notes on Eus. *H.E.* VI. 18. *The Church History
of Eusebius*, translated with prolegomena and notes (Library
of Nicene and Post-Nicene Fathers).

[2] Frag. of Pamphilus' and Eusebius' *Apology for Origen*,
quoted by McGiffert, *op. cit.* p. 396.

turned to his friends in Palestine, and settled at Caesarea, where he taught those who came to him for instruction; his fame was great; many pupils, we are told,[1] came to him not only from the vicinity, but crowds came from other countries. Among his pupils were Firmilian, Bishop of Caesarea in Cappadocia, Gregory Thaumaturgus, later Bishop of Caesarea in Pontus, and his brother Athenodorus. The presence of such a teacher, and of such pupils, must have given the Caesarean Church considerable intellectual respectability.

There was one person to whom Origen lectured in vain; Porphyry, the great Neo-Platonist, had heard Origen in his youth,[2] but had not been led to embrace the faith. He hated the allegorical explanations of the Jewish Scriptures and an unfortunate experience at the hands of some Caesarean[3] Christians would serve to confirm his hatred. The trouble was ἐπ᾽ ἰδιωτικοῖς πράγμασιν, and from this it was a mere step to the supposition that the great opponent of Christianity was φιλο-χρήματος.[4]

For over twenty years the work of the school

---

[1] Eus. *H.E.* vi. 30.   [2] Eus. *H.E.* vi. 19.

[3] Socrates, *H.E.* iii. 23. Harnack, 'The Fragments of Porphyry' (*Abhandlungen der königlich preussischen Akademie der Wissenschaften*, 1916), p. 37.

[4] Aristocritus in Harnack, *op. cit.* p. 40; cf. the treatment meted out to Natalius, the bishop of the 'Psilanthropists' at Rome, Eus. *H.E.* v. 28.

15

went on, broken by the persecution of Maximin,[1] in which Ambrose, the friend of Origen, and Protoctetus, a presbyter of Caesarea, suffered, and by the various expeditions which Origen made to suppress heresy—a task for which he seems to have been admirably fitted. He could save others but he could not save himself—controversy over him had started even in his lifetime.[2] At last the Decian[3] Persecution put an end to the school. Alexander of Jerusalem was martyred at Caesarea, and Origen, who had escaped for so long, was now, at the age of almost seventy, tortured. He died soon afterwards.

Three men[4] from the country flung their lives away in the Valerian Persecution by reckless display of their faith. A woman, a Marcionite, also suffered, but the historian has omitted to say whether she suffered by a like display of reckless-ness. After this the Church in general settled down to enjoy the 'long' peace, but before the final persecution one more martyr died at Caesarea— Marinus, a Roman soldier who preferred his faith to his military advancement.[5] A man of senatorial rank, Astyrius, acted the part of Joseph of Arima-thaea for the soldier martyr, who chose to serve a heavenly master when offered the choice by

---

[1] Eus. *H.E.* vi. 28.   [2] Eus. *H.E.* vi. 19.
[3] Eus. *H.E.* vi. 39, vii. 1.
[4] Eus. *H.E.* vii. 12.   [5] Eus. *H.E.* vii. 15.

Theotecnus the bishop.[1] Theotecnus, after a zealous tenure of the episcopal office, was succeeded by Agapius.[2] In the time of Agapius a young man was living and learning at Caesarea; Eusebius was his name, and he was to be the greatest churchman whom Caesarea had produced.

LIST OF BISHOPS OF CAESAREA

References are to the Historia Ecclesiastica *of Eusebius.*

A.D.
c. 190 Theophilus, *H.E.* v. 22.
c. 216 Theoctistus, *H.E.* vi. 19.
c. 259 Domnus, *H.E.* vii. 14 (for a short time).
c. 261 Theotecnus, *H.E.* vii. 14. (Theotecnus ordained Anatolius as his successor, but A., passing through Laodicea, yielded to the brethren there and became their bishop, vii. 32.)
c. 275 Agapius, *H.E.* vii. 32.
c. 313 Eusebius.

[1] Eus. *H.E.* vii. 16.
[2] Eus. *H.E.* vii. 32.

CHAPTER II

The Early Life and Environment of Eusebius, and his first Works

A Life of Eusebius was written by Acacius, his pupil and his successor as Bishop of Caesarea, but this work is completely lost.[1] Thus we are left without any coherent account of the life of Eusebius, and have to gain what knowledge of it we can from passages in his own works, and from the notices of him in contemporary and later writers. The latter type of reference is not very satisfactory, especially in the case of a man who was a leading churchman in a period of stormy theological controversy. Contemporaries are often not the best judges of a man's character, and the statements, guesses, and inferences of later writers are often coloured by the opinions which they themselves held. As we proceed, we shall see how difficult it is to make anything of the references to Eusebius, which are found in the ancient authors who deal with the period of the Arian controversy in which he lived (*c*. A.D. 318 onwards). The Arians wish to make him an Arian, the Orthodox are divided between denouncing his Arianism and saving the Father of Church History from the imputation of heresy.

The date and place of birth and the family of

---

[1] Socrates, *H.E.* II. 4; cf. Sozomen, *H.E.* III. 2, IV. 23.

Eusebius are unknown, but the first of these can be fixed with approximate accuracy. In the *Church History* he draws a distinct[1] line between his own and previous generations. This line is drawn after his account of Dionysius of Alexandria, but not before his mention of the death of that bishop,[2] which took place in the twelfth year of Gallienus (264–5). The latest date to which the letters of Dionysius quoted by Eusebius in his account refer is Easter of the year A.D. 262,[3] and other even which Eusebius places in the previous generation are the toleration[4] edict of Gallienus and the martyrdom of Marinus[5] at Caesarea, which took place when the Churches elsewhere were enjoying the peace which the toleration edict afforded. This martyrdom probably took place while the usurper Macrianus was still in power in the East, i.e. in 261–2.[6] With regard to the birth of Eusebius we must notice that the first events which he mentions as occurring in his own generation are the accession of Dionysius of Rome to the bishopric of that city and the accession of Paul of Samosata to the bishopric of Antioch; from some indication in his source Eusebius apparently recognised that these accessions stood near one another in point of time, as indeed they do. But Eusebius' reckoning

[1] *H.E.* VII. 26 fin. [2] *H.E.* VII. 28.
[3] Feltoe, *Dionysius of Alexandria*, pp. 69, 84. [4] *H.E.* VII. 13.
[5] *H.E.* VII. 15. [6] McGiffert, *op. cit.* p. 303, col. 2, note 1.

of the dates of the Roman bishops for this period is very faulty—according to his reckoning, Dionysius would become Bishop of Rome about A.D. 266, whereas it is generally agreed that 259[1] is the correct date, while Paul became Bishop of Antioch about 260.[2] It seems very improbable that Eusebius was born in 259 or earlier, owing to the fact that he dates such important events as the toleration edict of Gallienus and the martyrdom of Marinus —an important enough event for Caesarea—in the previous generation. We may therefore fix his birth between A.D. 262 and 265.

Of the place of his birth we have no knowledge: all that can be said is that Caesarea is the only place at which we know him to have lived; the appellations of 'Eusebius the Palestinian' or 'Eusebius Caesariensis' are no indication whatever of his native place; of his family we have no information. Of his race we can tell that he was not a Jew, but we do not know whether he was pure Greek or Greek with Syrian or other admixture. It seems to be generally assumed that he was a Christian born, not a Christian convert. With regard to this point there is little evidence one way or the other. But a passage[3] in the *Demonstratio Evangelica* may be

---

[1] McGiffert, *op. cit.* p. 401. Schwartz in Pauly-Wissowa, *Realenzyklopädie der klassischen Altertumswissenschaft*, art. 'Eusebios', col. 1370.   [2] Bardy, *Paul de Samosate*, p. 169.

[3] *D.E.* III. 4. 30, 31 (109 a).

noted; after a brief résumé of the marvellous[1] works of Christ, Eusebius says:

Such were the far-famed wonders wrought by the virtue of our Saviour, these were the proofs of His divinity; at these we ourselves also have wondered with reverent reasoning, and we have received these proofs with critical judgement after full trial and enquiry. We have enquired into these and have made trial of them, not only through other plain facts which make the whole subject clear, facts through which our Lord is accustomed to show even now, to those whom He thinks worthy, slight evidences of His power, but also by the more logical method which we are accustomed to use for the benefit of those who do not accept what has been said (i.e. the statements of the 'divine' works of Christ), but either completely disbelieve these proofs, and say that no such things were done by Him, or while admitting that these things happened, say that they were[2] done perversely by witchcraft for the deception of the spectators by Christ as by a fraud.[3]

It would be going too far to say, on the strength of this passage alone, that Eusebius had been a heathen. But the passage does seem to point to a personal experience of Eusebius: he had tried the

[1] In *D.E.* III. 4. 21 (107 c) Eusebius calls Christ παραδόξων ποιητὴς ἔργων—the phrase of Josephus. He uses this phrase in *H.E.* I. 2. 23 also.

[2] Read ἐπιτετέλεσθαι for ἐπίθεσθαι as Heikel suggests in his critical notes on this passage.

[3] W. J. Ferrar, *The Proof of the Gospel*, being the *Demonstratio Evangelica* of Eusebius of Caesarea, vol. I, p. 126 (with some alterations).

21

faith, and he had not found it wanting, he had studied it as revealed in the happenings of everyday life,[1] and as a proposition to which a logical proof was attached. In his apologetic works he is always insisting on the 'intellectual'[2] nature of Christianity, and his insistence on this point is all the more natural if he had reached his conception of the true faith by making trial of it for himself, rather than by receiving it blindly from the previous generation.

Eusebius, like many other men in all ages, owed everything to his teacher. If Pamphilus, a native of Berytus, a man of good family and of great learning, had not settled in Caesarea, the career of Eusebius might have been very different. Eusebius says[3] in the *Demonstratio Evangelica* that every master is better than his pupils. The actual reference is to Christ and His disciples, but can we doubt that Eusebius thought of his own master as he wrote?

Pamphilus had studied in the Christian school at Alexandria where Pierius had been his master;[4] thereafter he did not return to his native city, which, notwithstanding its reputation for secular learning, does not appear to have been a place[5] in which his talents as a Christian scholar could

---

[1] Cf. *Adv. Hieroclem*, c. 4, on the delivery of men's souls and bodies from malignant demons by the invocation of the name of Christ, ὡς αὐτοὶ πείρᾳ κατειλήφαμεν. [2] λογική.
[3] *D.E.* iii. 6. 8 (127 a). [4] According to Photius, *Cod.* 118.
[5] Cf. *Martyrs of Palestine*, 4. 3.

have found their proper level; he came to Caesarea, impelled, no doubt, by affection for Origen, his spiritual master, who had laboured so long there, and by the desire to collect and study the works of the great Alexandrian, some of which must have existed at Caesarea in his actual manuscript or in very early copies.

Pamphilus collected a library at Caesarea, and founded there a school of Christian instruction. From Caesarea as a centre the works of Origen and other Christian scholars would be disseminated through the Churches. Besides being a book collector, Pamphilus was a corrector of texts; he was especially anxious to fix the New Testament text of Origen,[1] who had, of course, himself made exhaustive researches into the various Greek versions of the Old Testament. Then other Churches would bring their copies of both Testaments to be corrected at Caesarea, and various surviving manuscripts still bear witness to the zeal of Pamphilus, which continued to the extreme limit of his life; 'I Pamphilus corrected the book in prison through the great grace and deliverance of God',[2] is one testimony to the work of the martyr, and other texts bear witness not only to his work, but to the work of Eusebius as well. The words τὸ Εὐσεβίου and τὸ Βιβλίον Εὐσεβίου τοῦ

[1] Schwartz in P.W. *loc. cit.* col. 1372.
[2] Schwartz, *loc. cit.* col. 1373. 1.

Παμφίλου often appear on manuscripts of the Old
Testament.[1] Another way in which the circle of
Pamphilus may have served the Church was by
making translations into other languages. Eusebius[2] mentions the fact that Procopius, who was
the first martyr at Caesarea in the Great Persecution, besides being reader and exorcist, served the
Church by translating from Greek into Aramaic.
Pamphilus was also most liberal in distributing texts
of the Scriptures to all who desired them.

> What lover of books was there who did not find a
> friend in Pamphilus? If he knew of any of them being
> in want of the necessaries of life he helped them to the
> full extent of his power. He would not only lend them
> copies of the Holy Scriptures to read but would give
> them most readily, and that not only to men, but to
> women also, if he saw that they were given to reading.
> He therefore kept a store of manuscripts, so that he
> might be able to give them to those who wished for
> them whenever occasion demanded.

Thus wrote Eusebius in the work which he composed on the life of his master, in a passage which
Jerome translated into Latin.[3]

[1] H. Leclercq, 'Eusèbe de Césarée', in Dictionnaire d'archéologie chrétienne et de liturgie, vol. v, 1, col. 749. Schwartz,
loc. cit. col. 1373.

[2] M.P. (long version). Cureton, Eusebius' Martyrs of Palestine, translated from the Syriac, p. 4. Lawlor and Oulton,
Eusebius, The Ecclesiastical History and the Martyrs of Palestine,
vol. I, p. 332.

[3] Jerome, Contra Ruf. 1. 9. Translated by Freemantle
(Nicene and Post-Nicene Fathers).

Eusebius speaks of Pamphilus in terms which show the utmost dependence on him; in one place he calls him 'the best loved of all my companions',[1] in another 'my lord Pamphilus, for by no other title can I rightly call the truly divine and blessed man'.[2] This title of 'my lord' is, no doubt, the origin of the sneer of Photius, 'Eusebius, whether slave or friend of Pamphilus, I know not'. There is no evidence that Eusebius was slave of Pamphilus other than this passage. That Pamphilus was regarded with the utmost affection by his servants is proved by the story of Porphyry,[3] the lad who did not wish the body of his master, on whom he had just heard sentence of death pronounced, to be thrown out for food to the beasts, but that Eusebius was Pamphilus' slave is not proven. One might as well say that Eusebius, Bishop of Nicomedia, had been a slave of Eusebius of Caesarea, because he calls him δεσπότης μου in a letter to Paulinus, Bishop[4] of Tyre. The word 'companion' does not suggest the relation of a slave to a master, while the name 'Pamphili' which Eusebius bore argues rather the position of an

[1] *M.P.* 7.
[2] *M.P.* (long version). Gr. frag. in *Analecta Bollandiana*, XVI. 129 ff., and in Schwartz' edition of the *H.E.* vol. II, p. 932, lines 7 ff.
[3] *M.P.* 11.
[4] Theodoret, *H.E.* I. 6.

25

adopted[1] son than of a freed man or merely a friend. A late author[2] would have it that Eusebius was nephew of Pamphilus, but this statement is unsupported by other evidence.

Through Pamphilus the influence of Alexandrian thought was brought to bear on Eusebius; it is necessary to note the fact that this thought did not take the form of undiluted Origen, but of Origen as he was interpreted by the scholars who succeeded him,[3] such as Dionysius or Pierius, with the latter of whom it is reasonable to suppose that Eusebius was well acquainted personally.[4] It was likewise through Pamphilus that Eusebius gained what knowledge he possessed of Greek philosophy and literature. But we must recognise that this scholars' paradise had its limitations; the field of Roman history was beyond its ken, Latin was almost a foreign tongue, the influence of Greek poetry was not apparent to any great extent in the works of Eusebius, of Hebrew these scholars had perhaps some, but not profound knowledge.

While remembering his intellectual duty to the Church Pamphilus did not forget the more practical side of Christianity.

[1] E. H. Gifford, *Eusebii Praeparatio Evangelica*, vol. III, part I, Introduction, pp. v–xi.   [2] Nicephorus, *H.E.* VI. 37.

[3] A point to be dealt with later: *infra*, chap. IV, pp. 86–88, 90.

[4] See *infra*, p. 29, note 1. Pierius wrote a *Life of Pamphilus* according to Philippus Sidetes, frag. 7 (De Boor in *Texte u. Untersuch.* vol. V. 2, p. 171 (1888)).

He[1] was a man distinguished through his whole life for every virtue, for his renouncing and despising this world, for his sharing his property with the needy, for his contempt of earthly hopes, for his ascetic rules and practices of life; especially did he excel all our generation in his most genuine devotion to the divine Scriptures, in his indefatigable industry in all undertakings, and in the help which he gave to his relatives and to those who came to him.

While ascribing the first place to Pamphilus among the friends of Eusebius, mention must be made of the other churchmen whom he knew or met in his youth. At the close of the seventh book of his *Church History* Eusebius devotes a long chapter[2] to the ecclesiastics of his own day: he did not know all whom he mentioned in that chapter, but as a young man he must have known many of them. In Caesarea he may possibly, though not probably, have known Theotecnus the bishop, who had been taught by Origen, though his mention of him is somewhat casual.[3] Agapius succeeded Theotecnus a considerable time before

---

[1] *M.P.* 11. 2.   [2] *H.E.* vii. 32.
[3] We must remember that Theotecnus had appointed Anatolius as his bishop coadjutor before A.D. 269, in which year Anatolius was carried off by the Church of Laodicea to be bishop there. It seems unlikely that Theotecnus would appoint a bishop coadjutor if he expected to have a long tenure of office, and it seems safer to place the accession of Agapius much nearer to the condemnation of Paul of Samosata than to the Great Persecution.

the outbreak of the Great Persecution. 'We know how hard Agapius worked, and that he exercised most genuine forethought in his oversight of the people, and cared particularly for all the poor with liberal hand'. It was more or less by accident that Agapius succeeded to the see of Caesarea. Theotecnus had marked out and ordained as his successor, Anatolius, an Alexandrian scholar, who was able, in troubles in his native city of Alexandria, to combine Aristotelian philosophy with diplomatic achievement.[1] But Anatolius did not succeed to his expected bishopric, for the Laodicean Church waylaid him while he was journeying to Antioch and made him their bishop, in succession to a friend of his, another Eusebius from Alexandria.

Our Eusebius is, indeed, very interested in the Church of the Laodiceans. He goes on to mention the successor of Anatolius, Stephen, a good scholar, but a renegade in the persecution: with Stephen is contrasted Theodotus, who restored the Church and on whom Eusebius lavishes every praise. Theodotus and Eusebius were close friends: and to Theodotus Eusebius dedicated two of his greatest works, the *Praeparatio* and *Demonstratio Evangelica*. We do not know when this friendship began, but the Bishop of Laodicea probably had, as we shall see later, a considerable influence on the actions of his friend of Caesarea.

[1] *H.E.* vii. 32.

28

Other churchmen were the Bishops of Antioch and Alexandria; of Antioch Cyril, with his learned presbyter Dorotheus, whom Eusebius had heard expounding the Scriptures in church, and of Alexandria, Maximus, and Theonas, and Peter, with Pierius[1] and Achillas the presbyters who continued the succession of Alexandrian scholars. Meanwhile Zambdas and Hermon were Bishops of Jerusalem, but Eusebius gives no details about them.

Other influences on Eusebius must have been at work as well. It must have meant something to him to have lived in a city where the Roman governor lived, and where the power of the Empire was an ever-present reality; his reverence for the actual benefits which the Empire conferred on mankind and even on the Church, by enabling its missionaries to have free access to all lands, was probably a legacy from his younger days. The Empire and the Church rose at the same time and the fact of the Empire enabled the Church to spread.

Who would[2] not agree that it was by God's providence (μὴ ἀθεεί) that the Empire synchronised in time with the teaching about our Saviour, when he realises

[1] Eus. *H.E.* vii. 32, uses the present tense with regard to Pierius, ἴσμεν...Πιέριον, and he places him ἐν τοῖς μάλιστα καθ' ἡμᾶς. Eusebius may also have known Faustus, a companion of Dionysius of Alexandria, who, an old man, was martyred in the Great Persecution (*H.E.* vii. 11).

[2] *D.E.* iii. 7. 33 (140 a, b).

29

that it was no easy task for His disciples to make their journeys to foreign[1] lands, when the nations were at variance with one another, and there was no intercourse because of the many different governments? When these were abolished the disciples accomplished their object fearlessly and safely, since the God of all made the way easy before them, and quelled the anger of the superstitious inhabitants of the cities, through fear of the great Empire.

In his later life Eusebius was destined to enjoy the favour of the ruler of the great Empire. Many years before that, however, he saw his future friend and benefactor in Palestine, when the young Constantine accompanied the Emperor Diocletian to Egypt in A.D. 296.[2] It seems very unlikely that Eusebius met Constantine on this occasion; if he had done so, he would certainly have pressed the point in writing the *Vita Constantini*, in which he is very anxious to make all that he can of his acquaintance with the subject of his work. It is, moreover, very improbable that Eusebius remembered much about Constantine's visit to Palestine when he wrote the *Vita* forty years later. The account of Constantine's appearance on that occasion is a recollection not of the Constantine of A.D. 296, but rather of the Constantine at the opening of the Council of Nicaea in A.D. 325.[3]

---

[1] Cf. his story about the difficulty of navigation in the civil wars in *H.E.* VIII. 15.

[2] *V.C.* I. 19.　　　　[3] Cf. *V.C.* I. 19 with III. 10.

In Caesarea, the Jews were also an ever-present
reality, and many a debate there must have been
between the learned men on the interpretation of
the prophecies. 'I remember', writes Eusebius,
'how I heard one of the circumcision saying...'[1]
—here is a brief reference to the insistence of
Jewish teaching that the prophecies had been
fulfilled long before Jesus was born, or were yet to
be fulfilled in the distant future. Again, in his
Commentary on Isaiah, a work of uncertain date,[2]
there are several references to Jewish interpretations of passages in the prophet which Eusebius
had heard from the mouth of the Rabbi. In one
case he is particularly explicit.[3] 'When I asked
and sought out the meaning of the passage at
present under discussion, the Rabbi said...', and
then follows the explanation. Coupled with these
constant brushes with Jewish scholarship, the fact
of living in Palestine filled Eusebius with feelings
of the greatest awe at the calamities which the Jews
had suffered for the rejection of Jesus.—'Who
would not wonder at this,[4] when one sees with

[1] *Eclogae Propheticae*, IV. 4 (p. 178, l. 16, Gaisford's edition).
[2] It was written later than the *Chronicle*. See *In Isaiam
xiii*. 17.
[3] *In Isaiam xxxix*. 1 ff. See also *In Isaiam xxiii*. 15, *xxxix*. 3.
Jerome, *Contra Ruf*. I. 13, refers to the use of Hebrew authorities by Origen, Clement, and Eusebius.
[4] *D.E.* VII. 1. 79 (324 d).

one's eyes the enemies of the Jews in possession of
every place in Judaea, and the foreigners and
idolaters settled at peace in all their cities and
districts?'—and again, 'you[1] will perceive the truth
of this if you think of Jerusalem, the once renowned
city of the Jewish race, with her glory and her
fruitfulness in God, now bereft of her holy citizens
and pious men'. Twice[2] he mentions, as a fact
of personal observation, the cultivation by the
Romans of part of Mount Zion; and he is touched
by seeing the stones from the temple of Jehovah
collected to build idol temples and theatres—a
σκυθρωπὸν θέαμα,[3] even to a Christian.

Though he lived in a seaport town, Eusebius
seems to have little interest in the sea; as far as we
know, he never made a journey by sea, and he
seldom mentions ships and sailors. We must remember that the interests of the average Christian,
whether man of letters or not, were much more
circumscribed than those of a Herodotus, for
instance. The studies of Eusebius were directed
entirely towards ecclesiastical affairs,[4] and thus his
outlook on life was one-sided. There is no record of
any extensive journeys on his part; we may be sure
that he knew the places connected with the life of

---

[1] *D.E.* vi. 7. 5 (265 b).
[2] *D.E.* vi. 13. 17 (273 d), viii. 3. 10 (406 c).
[3] *D.E.* viii. 3. 12 (406 d).
[4] Leclercq, *op. cit.* col. 762, brings this point out.

Jesus;[1] he may have visited Antioch and Alexandria in his youth, but we do not really know. His longer journeys were to be reserved for his old age, and the comfortable travelling facilities afforded by the generosity of the Emperor.

As we have noted above, the correction of texts was one of the leading literary occupations at Caesarea. It seems probable that this would be one of the earliest tasks on which Eusebius was engaged. It taught him accuracy, order,[2] neatness, and perseverance, qualities which seem to pursue him in his own works, in which so much consists in the transferring of passages from the text of his source to his own text. Moreover, may not a trait in Eusebius' character, which, late in his life, his theological opponent, Marcellus, mentions sarcastically, have its foundation in this work? Marcellus describes Eusebius as σφόδρα ἐπὶ τῷ μεμνῆσθαι τῶν γραφῶν μεγαλαυχῶν.[3]

Eusebius must have been a man of many note-books; even though much of the material treated by him in his voluminous works had been dealt with by earlier authors, he must have accumulated

[1] Caesarea Philippi, where the statue of Christ was, for instance. *H.E.* VII. 18. Bethlehem (*D.E.* I. I. 2, III. 2. 47 (97 c)) was a place of pilgrimage.
[2] Cf. Harnack, *Chronologie der altchristlichen Literatur*, vol. II, p. 107.
[3] Marcellus, *ap.* Eus. *Contra Marcellum*, I. 4. 60, as printed by Klostermann.

an enormous mass of notes and observations, which he used in the writing of his works, for the composition of some of these must be limited to quite short spaces of time in comparison with their length; the material must have been collected beforehand

Thus the life of Eusebius was a busy one, as his labours, from first to last, ranged over the whole field of literature. Apology, Chronology, History, Polemic, Panegyric, Sermons, Geographical work, are all included in his scope. Well has the author of the book 'on the Lights of the Church' remarked that 'we have never found anyone who could follow in all his footsteps'.[1] More recent times have added yet one more achievement to the literary labours of Eusebius, forgery. The imputation is a very natural one in the case of a man who quoted so much from sources, and no opportunity has been lost of raising the cry. Interpolation had been practised by Christians—in the works of Josephus, for instance—but the fact that Eusebius has preserved interpolated passages is no proof that he is the forger himself. The imputation of forgery gives Eusebius credit for far more cleverness than he possessed. His mind was essentially assimilative, not constructive. Moreover, as he was not blessed with the acumen of his critics he had no means of

[1] Quoted in the Testimonies in favour of Eusebius in Migne, *P.G.* vol. xix, col. 83. Translated in McGiffert, *op. cit.* p. 66.

deciding whether a historian named Sanchonia-thon[1] had ever existed in Phoenicia or not, or whether the works of Aristobulus[2] or the dramatist Ezekiel[3] were genuine. He used the texts to which he had access—sometimes perhaps not very good texts. Concerning the contemporary documents which he has included in his *Vita Constantini*, we stand on different ground; the problems connected with these documents will probably never be satisfactorily settled, but it seems unlikely that at the extreme end of his life Eusebius forged letters of a man whom he admired more than any other in a style so obscure as to be, in places, practically unintelligible.

Though Eusebius attempted so many branches of literature, we may be sure that his main interest was in Apologetics, not in Chronology or History for its own sake. His *Chronicle* is, of course, designed to show the antiquity of the Jews as compared with the Greeks and other races, but it is a Chronology released from the crudity of chiliastic forebodings, while the *History* is, consciously or unconsciously, a vindication of the Church against heretics and heathen.

In different works Eusebius sometimes uses the same arguments in almost the same words, without acknowledging his debt. Large passages are some-times transferred from one work to another: and

[1] *P.E.* I. 9. 20 ff. (30 d).
[2] *P.E.* VIII. 9. 38 (375 d), etc.   [3] *P.E.* IX. 28 ff. (436 d).

thus Eusebius might, in the course of his lifetime, use the same passage two, three or even four times. We do not really know what was the earliest work of Eusebius himself, but it seems likely that his work *Against Porphyry* was a youthful, and not too successful effort. Written originally in twenty-five books, it has perished with the exception of a few fragments; its loss is to be regretted chiefly because of the knowledge of Porphyry that we should have gained, even from the pen of an opponent. The detail given by Socrates[1] about Porphyry's unfortunate experience at the hands of some of the Caesarean Christians probably came from Eusebius, and the suggestion[2] that it was a feeling of local patriotism that caused Eusebius to write the work seems quite possible.

The work of Porphyry against the Christians was written about the year A.D. 270, and was proscribed by Constantine before the Council of Nicaea.[3] It is unlikely that Eusebius would write such a work after the proscription when the need would have vanished. Jerome, who had access to the library at Caesarea, does not appear to have seen Porphyry's work; no doubt the copy of Eusebius was committed to destruction enthusiastically

[1] Socrates, *H.E.* III. 23.
[2] Harnack, *op. cit.* vol. II, p. 119. Lightfoot, *Dictionary of Christian Biography*, art. 'Eusebius', p. 329.
[3] Harnack, Introduction to 'The Fragments of Porphyry', § 2.

in pursuance of the imperial command. But it does seem likely that the young scholar would be fired to write a reply to the man to whom Origen had lectured without avail in his own city of Caesarea. Eusebius never quotes from this work by name in any of his other writings. But we must remember that Eusebius has a habit of introducing long passages from earlier works of his own into later ones, without acknowledging the debt. Is it not possible that a considerable part of the *Demonstratio Evangelica* is taken from his work *Against Porphyry*? The third book of this work is probably the best thing that Eusebius ever wrote. It is directed against those who declared that Christ was a deceiver or a sorcerer, or that the account of His miracles was untrue. These topics had formed an important part of Porphyry's work.

It is probable that in refuting Porphyry Eusebius would adopt the method of Origen and pursue his opponent point by point. But his refutation was not regarded as a great work, and it was necessary for Apollinarius of Laodicea and for Philostorgius to write refutations as well. Philostorgius[1] is quite definitely of the opinion that the work of Apollinarius was much better than that of Eusebius and Jerome[2] seems to share this view; while the silence in which Eusebius has shrouded his effort would appear to confirm the suspicion that the work was

---

[1] *H.E.* p. 115, ed. Bidez. [2] *Ep.* LXXXIV. 2.

not a great success. There is not much objection
to placing such a long work at the beginning of
Eusebius' literary career; he was by nature verbose,
and a refutation of Porphyry, whose work extended
to fifteen books, would easily occupy twenty-
five books of Eusebius if the refutation of the
latter dealt with every point in Porphyry's work.

Much more important than the work *Against
Porphyry* is the *Chronicle*, which has given rise to
endless controversy among scholars. It is not
extant in the original Greek, but in a late Armenian
version and in the Latin version of Jerome, who
made additions to Eusebius' work in the field of
Roman history, of which Eusebius was very ignorant. Various Christians had written Chronicles
before the time of Eusebius; the aim of these had
been twofold:

1. The defence of Christianity against the
heathen who scoffed at its recent origin, by a
demonstration of the antiquity of the Jews, from
whom Christianity sprang, compared with that of
the heroes of the Greeks and other races.

2. An exposition of the time of the approaching
end of the world in accordance with Old and New
Testament prophecy.[1]

---

[1] Cf. Eus. *H.E.* VI. 7, where a chronographer Judas is
mentioned, who wrote on the seventy weeks in Daniel and
calculated that Anti-Christ was at hand in the tenth year of
Severus.

38

The first of these aims was the object of the work of Eusebius, but for the second he had no regard whatever. Chiliasm was an abomination to him. Of previous Christian chronographers the only one, probably, whom Eusebius used directly was Julius Africanus of Emmaus in Palestine, whose work, if we may believe Photius, dealt in summary fashion with events that had taken place in the Christian period. Eusebius could add many dates, or approximate dates, to the Chronicle of Africanus from his own reading. We can clearly see where his knowledge ended. It is bounded by language rather than by geography.[1] Latin seems to have been an almost insuperable obstacle to him, and it is remarkable evidence of the divergence between East and West, when one so learned as Eusebius was content to limit his knowledge in this way, and to glean what information he could about the Western Church from the notices of it in Greek writers.

The exact dates between which Eusebius compiled his *Chronicle* are unknown, but it is plain that the work was, in the first instance, an early one, though Jerome states in his Latin version that the work went up to the Vicennalia of Constantine, and the Armenian version, of which the end is lost, apparently was continued to this point, as the Vicennalia is mentioned in an earlier part of

[1] C. H. Turner, *Studies in Early Church History*, p. 139.

39

the work.[1] Eusebius mentions his *Chronicle* in the *Eclogae Propheticae*, the *Church History*, the *Praeparatio Evangelica*, and the *Commentary on Isaiah*.[2] These indications show that before the date of the works just mentioned the *Chronicle* was a completed work which in its original form did not, perhaps, extend so far as the events of the Great Persecution.[3] The *Church History* was an expansion of the *Chronicle*; in both we find the same information about the history of Christianity,[4] i.e. lists of bishops, information about the chief Christian prelates and writers, the heretics, the misfortunes of the Jews, the martyrs. But the last two topics with which the *Church History* dealt, (1) 'the martyrdoms of our own times', and (2) 'the gracious and kindly succour of our Saviour at the last', are an addition to the earliest plan of that work; they are added ἐπὶ τούτοις, 'in addition to' the above-mentioned list of topics, and since they are an addition to the *Church History*, it looks as

[1] J. Karst, *op. cit.* p. 62, l. 4. Schoene, *op. cit.* vol. I, p. 131, l. 8.

[2] References: *E.Pr.* I. 1; *H.E.* I. 1; *P.E.* x. 9; *Comm. in Isaiam xiii.* 13.

[3] Cf. the breviary of the Lemovicensian Church quoted by Valesius (Migne, *P.G.* vol. XIX, p. 82), Eng. transl. in McGiffert, *op. cit.* p. 66—which states, 'Scripsit quoque Chronicorum historiam a primo anno Abrahae usque ad annum trecentesimum, quam Hieronymus prosecutus est'. But this notice, taken by itself, seems very weak evidence.

[4] C. H. Turner, *op. cit.* p. 138. Eus. *H.E.* I. 1.

though they did not figure in the original form of the *Chronicle*.

There is little need to add here yet one more to the descriptions of the method and form of the *Chronicle*,[1] and it is also impossible in the present work to offer any solution of the weighty questions which surround the study of this work, questions such as 'Did Eusebius issue one or two editions of the *Chronicle*?' or 'Did Jerome use the genuine work of Eusebius or a revision of the genuine work by some misguided individual who attempted to fix dates for events to which Eusebius gives no definite dating in the *Church History*, and perverted dates which Eusebius knew correctly, as the *Church History* proves?' But the following suggestions may be made.

It is very unlikely that Jerome used the work of a reviser, who carried on the *Chronicle* to A.D. 326, whereas the original work had ended previous to A.D. 303, though correction, or supposed correction, of the *Chronicle* of Eusebius had begun by Jerome's time. Suidas mentions[2] that Diodorus,[3] Bishop of Tarsus in the time of Julian and Valens, wrote a

[1] For descriptions of the *Chronicle* of Eusebius see C. H. Turner, *op. cit.* pp. 135–41; C. H. Turner in *J. Th.S.* vol. 1; and J. K. Fotheringham's Introduction to his edition of Jerome's version.
[2] Quoted by Valesius (Migne, *P.G.* vol. xix, col. 97). Eng. transl. in McGiffert, *op. cit.* p. 72.
[3] Diodorus died before A.D. 394 (*D.C.B.* art. 'Diodorus').

Chronicle in which the errors of Eusebius were corrected. But it is most improbable that one who felt that he was improving the *Chronicle* of Eusebius —as the supposed reviser of Eusebius must have felt—would have pretended that his revision and addition (i.e. to 326) were still the original work of Eusebius. Jerome had no doubt about the *Chronicle* up to A.D. 326 being the work of the Bishop of Caesarea.

Nevertheless, the work between 303 and 326 was either not written very fully, or has had its original contents much altered by Jerome. Though the continuation deals with the period of the Great Persecution only one martyr is given by name,[1] one who is not mentioned by Eusebius in his *Church History*; Helena, mother of Constantine, is 'concubina', and the accession of that Emperor is described as 'Constantinus regnum invadit'. There is a notice of the 'Bellum Cibalense' of 314 between Constantine and Licinius, a war which Eusebius does not mention elsewhere; the notice about Lactantius may well be Jerome's own; the notice of the Council of Nicaea is certainly from Jerome —this is proved by the outspoken anti-Arian character of the notice, which cannot come from Eusebius, and by the fact that, whereas Eusebius

[1] Jerome, ed. Fotheringham, p. 311. The name of Basileus, Bishop of Amasia in Pontus, is given in the persecution of Licinius.

in the *Vita Constantini* gives 'over two hundred and fifty' as the number of the bishops, Jerome gives an exact 'three hundred and eighteen'. Moreover, Arianism, the faith of Eusebius' friends, is stigmatised as 'impietas' and the machinations of these heretics were brought to nought 'oppositione omoousii'. Eusebius, as we shall see later, was not the man to describe Arianism in such a way, or to give such credit to the term 'homoousios'. Then the death of Licinius is described as being 'contra ius sacramenti'; this phrase lays a second stigma on the imperial friend and patron of Eusebius, and finally the death or murder of the Emperor's eldest son and of the young Licinius his nephew is chronicled in a way in which Eusebius would never have allowed himself to write. In the *Vita Constantini* the only sentences that can refer to these terrible happenings are couched in the most tactful language possible.[1] There is therefore little left in the original work of Eusebius except the lists of bishops and the accessions and deaths of emperors; and with regard to these we have just seen how unlikely it is that the notice of the death of Licinius appears in Jerome as it did in the original *Chronicle* of Eusebius.

With regard to events dated exactly in the *Chronicle* but only approximately in the *Church History*, one can only say that it would be very

[1] *V.C.* I. 47. 2, IV. 54 fin.

43

improbable that Eusebius would use an approximate as opposed to an exact system of dating in the *Chronicle*, in which events were arranged under different years; in the *Church History* things are different, and the 'floruit', for instance, of a notable person could be conveniently placed in the reign of an emperor.

Discrepancies between the *Chronicle* and the *Church History* need not be referred to different hands at work. Eusebius is quite capable of changing a date himself, not only in separate works, but in the same book of the same work. In the tenth book of the *Praeparatio Evangelica* he gives expositions of the antiquity of the Jews, both from himself, and from Porphyry, Africanus, Tatian, Clement; finally he recurs to his own, and in the second exposition he places the fall of Troy in the time of the Jewish judge Eli, while in his previous one he had placed this event in the time of Labdon.[1] When we find such a discrepancy not in two separate works, but so close together in the same work, one must admit that Eusebius was very far from being an infallible chronological oracle.

[1] *P.E.* x. 9 (484 b), x. 14 (503 a).

CHAPTER III

The Great Persecution

Peace had brought many benefits to the Church, but it was not an unmixed blessing. Christians, as they increased in number, declined in quality, and when the threat of persecution was removed, they evinced little thankfulness for their changed situation, but spent their time in quarrelling with one another. Peace had brought laxity, sloth, envy, slander, hypocrisy, dissimulation, battles of words, outbreaks of bishop against bishop and congregation against congregation. Such is the melancholy catalogue which Eusebius[1] gives: he is probably thinking of individual cases, and his refusal to add details has made the forty years of the 'long' peace a dark chapter of *Church History*; while realising that such a state of things did exist, he feels[2] that it is so far from his own nature that he will not tell of it.

Eusebius regards persecution as brought about by the machinations of the powers of evil or of evil men, or as Heaven-sent chastisement for the sins of the Church. Curiously enough, in different

[1] *H.E.* VIII. 1.
[2] *H.E.* VIII. 2. 2, ...οὐχ ἡμῖν οἰκεῖον μνήμῃ παραδιδόναι....
Cf. *M.P.* 12, ἀνοίκειον ἐμαυτῷ κρίνας παραιτουμένῳ τε καὶ ἀποφεύγοντι...τὴν περὶ τούτων διήγησιν.

45

passages in his works, he states all these as causes of the Great Persecution of his own times. At the beginning[1] of his account he regards the affliction as sent to punish the Church for its wickedness; its arrival was not unheralded, if the bishops could have turned away from their own quarrels to perceive the signs of the coming storm. But later[2] he represents God as revealing by plague and pestilence His anger and indignation at all men for the great evils which they had brought on the Christians, and finally,[3] after peace had come, he regards the trials through which the Church had passed as the work of malignant envy and the evil-loving demon. Another idea of Eusebius is that the safety of the Empire and the peace of the Church go hand in hand; he comments several[4] times on the misfortunes that came about after persecution had begun, compared with the prosperity which had enriched the first nineteen years of Diocletian's reign. There seems, at first sight, a contradiction between this idea and the idea that persecution was a Heaven-sent chastisement for the sins of the

[1] *H.E.* VIII. 1. 8; cf. *M.P.* 13. 12. The Church in the West escaped lightly in the persecution, owing to the single-heartedness and faith of its members. It may further be noted that the Great Persecution is the only one which Eusebius regards as the work of God (E. Keller, *Eusèbe, Historien des Persécutions*, pp. 47, 77).

[2] *H.E.* IX. 8. 15.   [3] *H.E.* x. 4. 14.

[4] *H.E.* VIII. 13. 9, VIII. 14. 18.

46

Church. Should the Empire, the minister of divine vengeance on a recalcitrant Church, be therefore involved in grievous troubles? With regard to this point Eusebius has really much the same outlook as the prophets in the Old Testament. The idea is clearly set forth there that Assyria, Babylon, and Chaldaea, the ministers of God's anger on His people, are nevertheless to be destroyed.[1]

Before proceeding to an account of the experiences of Eusebius in the persecution it will be well to mention briefly the two accounts of it which he wrote. In the first place he has given a general account with little specific detail in the eighth book of his *Church History*; in the second place he wrote a work entitled *The Martyrs of Palestine*, which is, naturally, much more detailed with regard to conditions in a single province, and which exists in two versions, the shorter of which is extant in Greek, and the longer in Syriac and in Greek fragments.

In these two works, Eusebius gives two different dates for the promulgation of the first edict against the Christians. The exact date of its original appearance in Nicomedia is, as we know from Lactantius, the 23rd of February, A.D. 303.[2] From that date onwards, other provinces received the edict at varying intervals, according to their

---

[1] Isaiah x. 5 ff. (Assyria), Jeremiah xxv. 1–14 (Babylon), Ezekiel xxxi. 3–18 (Assyria), Habakkuk i and ii (Chaldaea).
[2] *De Mort. Pers.* 12.

47

distance from Nicomedia. In the eighth book of his *Church History* Eusebius gives[1] the month of March, 'when the festival of our Saviour's passion was approaching', for the date; in the *Martyrs of Palestine*[2] he gives 'the month of April at the time[3] of the festival of our Saviour's passion'. In the first-mentioned book Eusebius states that he was an eye-witness of the carrying out of the provisions of the edict, of the destruction of churches, and of the burning of the Scriptures. But in the *Martyrs of Palestine*, which is intimately connected with his own Church of Caesarea, he does not say anything about these happenings.

If we take the view that the 'long' version of the *Martyrs of Palestine* is earlier than the shorter form, it becomes indeed doubtful whether the church or churches in Caesarea were ever destroyed, because, in the 'long' version it is stated[4] that the bodies of Pamphilus and of those who were martyred with him were exposed for four days and nights, to be devoured by wild beasts, but, as these did not touch the bodies, they were taken up by the Christians and after the usual rites were laid in the customary tomb—in the churches, which must have been

[1] *H.E.* VIII. 2. 4, τῆς τοῦ σωτηρίου πάθους ἑορτῆς ἐπελαυνούσης.

[2] *M.P.* Prologue.

[3] ἐπιλαμβανούσης.

[4] Greek text in Schwartz' edition of the *H.E.* vol. II, p. 945.

standing when Eusebius wrote this. The short
version of the *Martyrs* says nothing about churches,
but merely that the bodies were laid in the
customary tomb. Notwithstanding the weight of
authority[1] which supports the view that the 'long'
version is the earlier, the increased information in
that version looks like the product of the author's
imagination rather than reasoned statements
written soon after the events actually took place.
In the capital city of a province it is very unlikely
that the churches would escape destruction.

A probable explanation of the double dating is
that Eusebius was not at Caesarea when the persecution broke out and that the early date, March,[2]
is the month in which he had himself heard the
proclamation, while the later date, April,[3] was the
month in which it was issued in Caesarea; April is
therefore the natural date for Eusebius to give, in
the account of the local persecution, the *Martyrs of
Palestine*. Wherever he was, he saw the actual
carrying out of the edict. We cannot fix the spot
where Eusebius heard the persecution proclaimed
in March, but it must have been nearer Nicomedia
than Caesarea was. A visit to Antioch[4] might

---

[1] Of Cureton, *op. cit.* Introduction, Lightfoot in *D.C.B.*
vol. II, pp. 320 f., and Lawlor, *Eusebiana*, pp. 279 ff. Schwartz
in P.W. *loc. cit.* col. 1408, takes the opposite view, as does
Leclercq, *loc. cit.* col. 765.
[2] I.e. in *H.E.* VIII.   [3] I.e. in *M.P.* chap. I.
[4] Cf. Schwartz in P.W. *loc. cit.* col. 1373, l. 21.

49

be a possibility. Eusebius had heard Dorotheus,[1] the learned presbyter of that Church, who was one of the earliest martyrs at Nicomedia, expounding the Scriptures, but whether he heard him on a visit just before the persecution or not, it is impossible to say.

Persecution at Caesarea was very spasmodic; it was vigorously enforced during less than three out of ten and a half years,[2] and during its whole course not one of the Palestinian bishops was put to death. More stringent edicts or more severe officials were constantly needed to ensure any sort of continued attempt to sweep the Church away; and, no doubt, new governors tried new methods.

What did Eusebius do in the persecution? He has given us a few hints in the eighth book of the *Church History* and in the *Martyrs of Palestine*, while one or two indications can be gathered from other sources. At some period of the persecution he visited Tyre,[3] and the Thebaid.[4] These visits seem to have taken place after the issue of the third edict, enjoining torture on imprisoned clergy who refused to sacrifice, and before the introduction of

---

[1] There seems no need to postulate two men of that name as McGiffert does, *op. cit.* p. 323.

[2] Lawlor, *Eusebiana*, p. 210. Ten and a half years from the first edict of Diocletian to the final edict of Maximin.

[3] *H.E.* VIII. 7. 1.   [4] *H.E.* VIII. 9. 4.

the edict substituting mutilation for death, which
was issued about A.D. 307.[1] On both these visits
Eusebius was the eye-witness of martyrdoms; at
Tyre he witnessed the contest of the martyrs with
wild beasts, and the miraculous reluctance of the
animals to touch them; in the Thebaid he saw many
Christians put to death in a single day, some by
fire, others by the sword; so many were there that
the sword was blunted and the executioners were
worn out.

About the end of 307 a severe blow was dealt at
the Church of Caesarea. Pamphilus was arrested,
tortured, and thrown into prison, where he re-
mained for two entire years. 'Urbanus—the
governor—first made trial of him in philosophy and
rhetoric, and later attempted to compel him to
sacrifice, and when he saw that Pamphilus took no
account of his threats, finally he became enraged
and ordered him to be tortured with the severest
tortures'.[2] Was Eusebius arrested at the same
time?

Many years later, at the Council of Tyre in
A.D. 335, at which Eusebius was presiding, an
Egyptian bishop named Potammon[3] taunted him,

[1] *M.P.* 7. 3, on November 5th, 307, mutilation of Silvanus
and others in fifth year of the persecution, i.e. 307–8; cf.
Adversus Hieroclem, 4 and 19, and *infra*, p. 71.

[2] *M.P.* 7.

[3] Epiphanius, *Haer.* LXVIII. 8, as translated by McGiffert,
op. cit. p. 9; cf. Athanasius, *Apol. contra Arianos*, 8.

saying that they had been together in prison during the persecution, and that whereas he (Potammon) had lost an eye for the truth, Eusebius had got off scot-free. How could Eusebius have escaped unless he had committed some dishonourable act? Who was he that he should sit in judgement on the innocent Athanasius? Eusebius rose and adjourned the meeting saying, 'If you come hither, and make such accusations against us, then do your accusers speak the truth. For if you tyrannise here, much more do you in your own country'. The fact of the accusation does not rest on the testimony of Epiphanius alone, for it is also mentioned in a letter of the Catholic Egyptian bishops on behalf of Athanasius;[1] in cataloguing the iniquities of those who composed the Synod of Tyre they say: 'Was not Eusebius of Caesarea in Palestine accused of sacrificing by the confessors who were with us?' The charge is not pressed: the passage concerned is merely a summary list of the disqualifications of the enemies of Athanasius, but we must not therefore dismiss it.

Now every persuasion, and sometimes even force was used in the attempt to save the lives of the Christians. The sacrificing was often a mere formality from the religious point of view. Christians were dragged to the altars, their cries were silenced by blows and they 'sacrificed' and were let go.

[1] Contained in Athanasius, *Apol. contra Arianos*, 3 ff.

Such persons were obviously not 'lapsi' in the proper sense: they were just as loyal to the faith as the bravest of the martyrs, and it would give considerable pleasure to the soldiers to compel them to do such a distasteful thing—more pleasure, perhaps, than to torture them. If Eusebius sacrificed willingly in the persecution, his works are a witness to consummate hypocrisy on his part; in these he shows striking admiration for the martyrs, while feeling sympathy with those whose faith did not stand the test.[1] It is not likely that soon after peace was restored a 'lapsed' Christian would be made Bishop of Caesarea, but there seems no reason why an unwilling sacrificer should not have been promoted. The instances which Eusebius gives in the *Church History* and in the *Martyrs of Palestine* of unwilling sacrifice seem to belong to the beginning of the persecution, but we can see that such methods were quite likely at a later period. They attempted to compel Pamphilus to sacrifice.

Before the time of the imprisonment of Pamphilus we do not hear of any Egyptian[2] confessors in Palestine. But in the sixth year of the persecution (i.e. 308–9) the authorities began to send batches of confessors from Egypt to the mines in

[1] See *E.Pr.* p. 231, l. 3 (Gaisford).
[2] Except two whom Eusebius names in *M.P.* 3. 3. But these two were not deported from Egypt to the mines.

53

other provinces. At Caesarea a large batch[1] was mutilated and sent to work at Phaeno. This took place during the imprisonment of Pamphilus. Eusebius also mentions Egyptian confessors who were seized at the gates of Caesarea on their return from visiting the Christians who had been deported to the mines in Cilicia.[2] It seems quite probable that Potammon and Eusebius should have met in prison. The fact that during the imprisonment of Pamphilus five books of the *Defence of Origen*[3] were written by Eusebius and Pamphilus in conjunction is not a strong argument in favour of the imprisonment of Eusebius with his master. That it was easy for Christians to have access to their imprisoned friends is shown by the fact that Pamphilus had corrected the parent of one surviving manuscript in prison and may have corrected others.[4] The *Defence of Origen* could have been written equally well whether Eusebius was a prisoner or not.

On February 16th, A.D. 310, Pamphilus was martyred[5] by beheading, with eleven others; five of these were Egyptians, who were returning from a visit to the confessors in the Cilician mines, three, of whom Pamphilus was one, had been in prison at Caesarea, while the other four flung their lives

---

[1] *M.P.* 8. 1.   [2] *M.P.* 10. 1.
[3] Photius, *Cod.* 118.
[4] Cf. *supra*, p. 23.   [5] *M.P.* 11.

away unnecessarily. With the death of Pamphilus his mantle passed to Eusebius.

The mines at Phaeno have already been mentioned. Among the mutilated confessors,[1] there was a number of men whom age and hardship had incapacitated from work. One of these was named John, an Egyptian, who had been blinded, and 'in the excellence of his memory surpassed all those of my time'. Eusebius declares that on one occasion he was astonished at hearing the repetition of the Scriptures by the confessor who, with a considerable number of Christians standing round, recited them to his hearers. At first Eusebius thought that the man was reading but when he came near he found out the truth, and he uses the blind confessor as an example of a great spirit triumphing over bodily disabilities. Did Eusebius visit the confessors at the mines? In the Syriac version of the *Martyrs of Palestine* he mentions the fact that many people visited the Christians there and did them acts of kindness.[2] Moreover, the *Defence of Origen* was dedicated to the Egyptian confessors at Phaeno,[3] who had shown themselves partisans of the anti-Origen reaction at Alexandria in the early fourth century. As John was among

[1] *M.P.* 13.
[2] Cureton, *op. cit.* p. 46. Lawlor and Oulton, *op. cit.* p. 396.
[3] Rufinus, transl. of book I, Preface (Migne, *P.G.* vol. xvii, col. 542).

those martyred in the vindictive attack of Maximin on these helpless cripples,[1] Eusebius must therefore have heard him recite the Scriptures while the persecution was yet going on, and he gives no indication that he heard him at Caesarea. So a visit to Phaeno towards the end of the persecution seems probable. Thus with regard to the movements of Eusebius in the persecution, we find that it may be reasonably suggested that he was absent from Caesarea in March, 303, that he made visits to Tyre and the Thebaid before 307, that he was imprisoned for some time, whether long or short we know not, between the end of 307 and the beginning of 310, and paid a visit to Phaeno, after completing the *Defence of Origen*, between the time of the death of Pamphilus in February, 310, and the issue of the Palinode of Galerius in April, 311.

Peace came to the Church, and all the Christians rejoiced,[2] notwithstanding the doubtful assent of Maximin to the change of policy, but their rejoicing was soon cut short. The heathen population of various cities petitioned[3] Maximin first to prevent the Christians from meeting in the cemeteries, and then to expel them from the several cities. Eusebius states that this stroke of policy was

---

[1] Cureton, *op. cit.* p. 48. Lawlor and Oulton, *op. cit.* p. 399. *M.P.* (Greek), 13. Eusebius does not actually say that John was martyred but it seems very likely.

[2] *H.E.* IX. 1.   [3] *H.E.* IX. 2.

engineered by Maximin himself, and there seems
to be no reason to doubt this statement; even if the
request was spontaneous, Maximin must have been
already preparing for his final assault on the
Church. The methods of propaganda which he
now proceeded to employ instead of the old-
fashioned frontal attack with fire and sword were
too subtle to be evolved overnight. His idea of
setting up a pagan in opposition to the Christian
Church was the best stroke that a persecutor ever
made; if the plan had had time to become properly
effective, the final peace of the Christians might
have been indefinitely removed, though one cannot
doubt that they would have beaten their pagan
opponents eventually. The weak spot in Maximin's
scheme was his adoption, as the 'Pagan Scriptures', of the *Acts of Pilate* which contained blas-
phemies against Christ—on such a negative basis
a pagan church could not have flourished.

The old methods of persecution were not entirely
given up. A sudden attack[1] was made on the
bishops and leaders of the Church—shall we say
on the most influential teachers at that moment,
on Peter, Bishop of Alexandria, and on Lucian,
the brilliant scholar of Antioch? These two and
others in different places were put to death. This
spasm of persecution does not appear to have
touched Caesarea. Eusebius could not have failed

[1] *H.E.* ix. 6.

57

to mention it, as the pestilence and famine which took place in the winter of 312–13 seem to have affected Palestine severely, and various phrases used by Eusebius indicate that he was an eye-witness[1] of these calamities; the bodies lying un-buried for many days were a pitiable sight to 'those who saw them', in all places one could see nothing but funerals, and sometimes two or three bodies being carried from one house at once: one interesting detail is the mention of the tax lists on which the taxable population had been almost wiped out. Perhaps the severity of these evils, by filling the hands of the officials, saved the Caesarean Church from persecution.

In the midst of these miseries the Church, though under a ban, showed itself at its best.

For instance, alone in such a crisis of evil they showed by deeds sympathy and humanity. Every day some continued gallantly caring for and burying the dead bodies—and there were crowds of these which had no one to attend to them; others collected in one place those who were pressed by hunger throughout the whole city (i.e. Caesarea) and distributed bread to all; the fact became noised abroad to all men, and they glorified the God of the Christians, and, convinced by the facts themselves, confessed that the Christians alone were truly pious and religious.[2]

[1] *H.E.* IX. 8. The famine and pestilence were probably local: no other writer mentions them except Lactantius vaguely, in a single sentence (*De Mort. Pers.* 37).

[2] *H.E.* IX. 8. 14.

Persecution had broken friendships for Eusebius and made new ones. Meletius,[1] Bishop of the Churches in Pontus, hid from the fury of the persecution during seven years in the regions of Palestine. Eusebius knew him—those whom he taught called him τὸ μέλι τῆς 'Αττικῆς. His great learning would be apparent if you tried him even once. Among the martyrs in the persecution was a young man named Apphianus,[2] of high-born pagan parents, from Pagae in Lycia. He could not abide his pagan relations, ran away from home, and in his wanderings came to Caesarea, where he was a very close friend of Eusebius, and studied and lived in the same house with him. But their friendship was of short duration, for, in super-abundant enthusiasm for the faith, Apphianus determined to accost the governor in person. He seems to have done this by plan and not by a sudden impulse. Eusebius says that he had told no one, 'including myself who lived in the same house', of his intention, which involved the evasion of the guards of the governor, but unexpectedly seized the hand of Urbanus and prevented him from sacrificing. Such insolence merited the reward which it received, though Eusebius seems to have approved the rashness of the deed.[3] Apphianus,

---

[1] *H.E.* VII. 32. 27.   [2] *M.P.* 4.

[3] On the other hand, Eusebius does not approve of the action of the Christian who tore down the proclamation at

after being tortured on two separate days, was cast into the sea.

As for what happened immediately afterwards, it is not unlikely that those who did not see it will disbelieve; however, though I know that this will be the case, I cannot but add the story in full to my narrative, because, to speak plainly, all the inhabitants of Caesarea were witnesses of the happening. There was really no age that did not behold this marvellous sight. The martyr had just been cast into the sea when an earthquake occurred and a commotion of the waters, and his body was cast out on the shore. Such is the account of Eusebius in the short version of the *Martyrs of Palestine*; in the long[1] version the scene is much more vivid; how the crowd of all ages and ranks ran together to see the body of the martyr!

There was one other miracle which astonished[2] the Caesareans. Firmilian the governor had ordered the bodies of the martyrs to be thrown to the beasts of prey, and the disgusting sight was exhibited of torn human limbs lying outside the city—some said that they had seen them even inside. As though in mute protest, a miraculous

Nicomedia at the beginning of the persecution (*H.E.* VIII. 5). The difference between the two cases is, that the action at Nicomedia was simply an insult to the government, while Apphianus was dealing a blow at the evil demons (Keller, *op. cit.* p. 57).

[1] Cureton, *op. cit.* p. 17. Lawlor and Oulton, *op. cit.* p. 352.
[2] *M.P.* 9.

sweat appeared on the buildings of the city, although the sky was clear and there was no mist. The phenomenon was apparently obvious enough to cause consternation in the inhabitants. Eusebius again adds that this story will appear a silly myth to later days, ἀλλ' οὐχ οἷσπερ ὁ καιρὸς τὴν ἀλήθειαν ἐπιστώσατο.

There is no reason to disbelieve either of these miracles which were brought to pass, we may be sure, by natural causes. The miraculous element is not one which bulks largely in Eusebius' works; this element in Christian literature grew as the Church became older, and apparently more imaginative.

It was a curious thing that the library at Caesarea was not destroyed in a time when Christian books were sought after: the haul of texts of the Scriptures in the library would have been a richer one than the search of many churches would have yielded, but the intelligence of the persecuting officials seems to have been limited to the devising of new methods of torture for individual Christians. The years of the persecution were years of continuous literary labour on the part of Eusebius, culminating in the work by which his name has become most famous, *The Church History*.

To try to fix exact dates for all the works which Eusebius wrote is to put one's self into the position of the supposed reviser of the *Chronicle*; the most that can be done is to give approximate datings, and to make suggestions; one danger that must be avoided is that of cramming several important works into a very short space of time. Even if Eusebius had collected much of his material beforehand, one cannot but imagine that long works like the *Praeparatio* and *Demonstratio Evangelica* would take a considerable time to produce, notwithstanding the extraordinary industry of their author, and the fact that quotation bulks so largely in them.

The *General Elementary Introduction* must have been written partly at any rate during the persecution. Of this work Books vi to ix[1] are extant under the title of *Eclogae Propheticae*; these four books, although included in the larger work, nevertheless are regarded by Eusebius himself as constituting an independent production.[2] In the Caesarean Church, which placed a high value on intellectual attainment, and which sought to keep up a school on the lines of the Alexandrian one, a manual of instruction for the use of teachers and pupils would be very necessary. The *General Elementary Introduction* aims at covering the whole ground of Christian instruction and at defending the progressing faith of the convert against the arguments of Jews and heretics.

We do not know how many books the original

---

[1] Book ii of the *Eclogae Propheticae* is incomplete. See H. Smith in *J. Th.S.* vol. xviii, p. 78.   [2] *E.Pr.* iii, Preface.

work comprised; at the end of Book IV of the *Eclogae Propheticae* Eusebius announces[1] his intention of writing a tenth book of the whole work in which he will provide an approach to the faith for the heretics, whose reason has been corrupted—we cannot say, however, whether Eusebius regarded the tenth book as completing his work. The part of the work directed against the heretics would largely, we may presume, be a defence of the Old Testament against such heretics as rejected it—against the Marcionites, for instance, who had followers in Palestine,[2] and perhaps even in Caesarea[3] itself.

Eusebius has told us something about the contents of the first five books. The mutilated first sentence of Book I of the *Eclogae Propheticae* states that the author had gone through the evidence of the teaching and the life of Christ, and had established it by clear, straightforward and true proofs, and had given at the end a short selection of evidence from the Jewish Scriptures. It is likely that this section of the work was founded in part at any rate on Eusebius' work *Against Porphyry*, and contained much of the material of the third book of the *Demonstratio Evangelica*, which was probably the best thing that Eusebius ever wrote. It is to be noticed in this connection that whereas there are many reminiscences of the *Eclogae Propheticae* in

[1] *E.Pr.* IV. 35 fin.   [2] *M.P.* 10.   [3] *H.E.* VII. 12.

63

the other extant books of the *Demonstratio*, there are only one or two in the third. This book does not deal with prophetic passages, but is a defence against those who said that Christ was a deceiver, or who attacked the trustworthiness of the Gospel narrative, and Eusebius must have gone over much if not all of his material in these lost books.

These first five books were for the use of ἀκροώ-μενοι,[1] a class to be initiated[2] into the first elements of the letter of the four Gospels. There was no point in overloading the first instruction of would-be Christians with Old Testament prophecies, in which they might find difficulty in believing. The *Eclogae Propheticae* were for the use of catechumens[3] and believers and comprise a defence of Christian as against Jewish exegesis: Book I deals with passages from the Historical Books, Book II with passages from the Psalms, Book III with passages from the Poetic Books and the Prophets, and Book IV with passages from Isaiah.

Whatever may have been the state of affairs during the writing of the first five books, the Church was certainly being persecuted while Eusebius was composing the *Eclogae Propheticae*, and there was little hope of a cessation[4] of persecution. The work

---

[1] *E.Pr.* I. 1 (p. 1, l. 6, Gaisford).
[2] *H.E.* x. 4. 63; cf. *D.E.* VII. 2. 52 (350 b).
[3] *E.Pr.* p. 3, l. 1 (Gaisford).
[4] *E.Pr.* p. 219, ll. 16 ff. (Gaisford).

has been dated about 303–5[1] or about 310.[2] The earlier date seems more suitable, though it is by no means certain; about 310 the output of work by Eusebius was very great, and it seems hard to burden this busy period with a production of this length. The *Eclogae Propheticae* mentions the *Chronicle* as already finished,[3] and is itself mentioned in the *Church History*; these references fix its date within wide limits.

Photius[4] cites as works of Eusebius a *Praeparatio Ecclesiastica* in which there are *Selections*, and a *Demonstratio Ecclesiastica*. The number of books is obliterated in both cases. From the reference to *Selections* (ἐκλογαί), it has been suggested[5] that the *Praeparatio Ecclesiastica* is the same as the *General Elementary Introduction*. There is little other evidence concerning the *Praeparatio* and *Demonstratio Ecclesiastica*, the existence of which is somewhat nebulous, as the only other reference to them which we have gives no indication of the contents.[6] The allusion in the *Praeparatio Evangelica*[7] to a work in which Eusebius had collected multitudes of other sayings

[1] Harnack, *Chronologie*, II. 114.
[2] Schwartz in P.W. *loc. cit.* col. 1387. 11 ff. There are, according to Schwartz, references to deportees, 'lapsi', and Pamphilus, on pp. 230–1 of Gaisford's edition of *E.Pr.*
[3] *E.Pr.* p. 1, l. 27 (Gaisford).   [4] *Cod.* 11, 12.
[5] By Schwartz, P.W. *loc. cit.* See also Lightfoot, *D.C.B.* art. 'Eusebius', p. 331.
[6] Mentioned by Lightfoot, *loc. cit.*   [7] *P.E.* I. 3. 12.

and prophecies of our Saviour, setting the fulfilments beside His divine foreknowledge, has been
referred[1] to the *Demonstratio Ecclesiastica*, but it
seems probable that it points to the lost books of
the *General Elementary Introduction*.

As has already been mentioned, Pamphilus and
Eusebius wrote a *Defence of Origen* during the imprisonment of Pamphilus, to which Eusebius added
one book after the death of the martyr. The cause
of writing was the attacks on Origen by opponents
whom Eusebius describes as 'the contentious';[2] to
read Origen seems to have been regarded in certain
circles as a theological crime of the greatest mag-
nitude. The work was dedicated to the Egyptian
confessors in the mines in Palestine who were
affected by the anti-Origen tendency.

Methodius, in his works *On the Resurrection* and
On Free Will, had attacked Origen, and, according
to Jerome,[3] he was attacked by Eusebius in the sixth
book of the *Defence*, the production of Eusebius
alone. Whether the attack of Methodius was the
direct cause of the writing of the *Defence* or not we
do not know: when Pamphilus was arrested, it probably seemed to him that the situation with regard
to the orthodoxy of Origen was too serious for delay.
The peril in which he stood made haste impera-
tive, and so it came about that Pamphilus, who

---

[1] By Lightfoot, *D.C.B. loc. cit.*   [2] *H.E.* VI. 33 fin.
[3] Jerome, *De Vir. Ill.* 83; *Contra Ruf.* I. 11.

66

wrote little, according to Jerome,[1] turned with the assistance of Eusebius to acquit Origen of the charges which perversity and ignorance had brought against him. Perhaps other literary work was dropped in order to allow the *Defence* to proceed.

The *Defence* contained some biographical as well as dogmatic material. In the *Church History*, Eusebius twice[2] refers his readers to it for further information with regard to the life of Origen, about which the older contemporaries of Eusebius could tell much, from oral tradition. But oral tradition sometimes did not coincide with the documentary evidence of the letters of Origen of which Eusebius had made a collection,[3] and we find that, in his account of Origen's sufferings previous to his death, Eusebius followed the letters[4] though the other account from Pamphilus and oral tradition was also allowed to stand.

Jerome at first believed[5] that both Pamphilus and Eusebius had written separate works in defence of Origen, though he had not read either.[6]

---

[1] *Contra Ruf.* i. 9, ii. 23, relying on the *Life of Pamphilus* by Eusebius.

[2] *H.E.* vi. 23, vi. 36.   [3] *H.E.* vi. 36.

[4] Photius suspected the genuineness of these last letters of Origen: εἴ γε αἱ φερόμεναι αὐτοῦ μετὰ τὸν Δεκίου διωγμὸν ἐπιστολαὶ οὐκ ἔχουσι τὸ πλαστόν. (Quoted in P.W. *loc. cit.* 1385. 39 ff.)

[5] Cf. *De Vir. Ill.* 75 with 81.   [6] *Contra Ruf.* ii. 23.

About A.D. 397 Rufinus translated the first book of the *Defence* into Latin and in the heading ascribed it to Pamphilus alone. When the question of the orthodoxy of Origen became pressing, Jerome read the book ascribed to Pamphilus in Rufinus' translation—he admits[1] that he had never seen the supposed *Defence* of Pamphilus in the original Greek—and also the six books of the *Defence* in Greek, and, of course, he found that Rufinus' translation coincided with the first of the six books which Jerome supposed to be the work of Eusebius, except that he accuses Rufinus of altering some heretical passages. Jerome says that in the library at Caesarea he found a copy of the six books which bore the name of Eusebius alone,[2] and he accuses Rufinus of dishonouring the memory of the martyr Pamphilus by making him the defender of a heretic—the work was that of Eusebius alone who 'in six volumes does nothing else than show Origen to be of his own faith, that is, of Arian perfidy'. But in view of Eusebius' definite statement of joint authorship it seems hardly necessary to take Jerome seriously.

Eusebius commemorated the life of Pamphilus in a work extending to three books which is completely lost, except for a single fragment. This was written before the initial form of the *Church History*,

<hr/>

[1] *Contra Ruf. loc. cit.*   [2] *Contra Ruf.* III. 12.

and the *Martyrs of Palestine*, and after the death of
Pamphilus in February, A.D. 310. It was not only
laudatory in its scope, but embraced the whole life
of Pamphilus. When Eusebius tells us what he
intends to do, or not to do in a work, he sticks to his
statement in the work itself. Of Pamphilus he says,
'I have described, in my special work about him,
all the particulars of his life, and of the school which
he established; his trials in different confessions
during the persecution, and the crown of martyrdom with which he was finally honoured'.[1] This
may be taken as a fair statement of the contents
of the work. One other detail about the contents
has been preserved by Eusebius: in it there was a
catalogue of the works of Origen and other ecclesiastical writers in the library of Pamphilus. If this
had been preserved it would have thrown interesting light on the extent of the literary knowledge
of Eusebius: we should be able to detect whether
he is quoting from actual works or from quotations
in some earlier author. This *Life of Pamphilus*, and
the one by Pierius, are the oldest Greek Christian
biographies of which we know,[2] and therefore are
milestones in Christian literary history, though in
Latin Pontius' *Life of Cyprian* had already forestalled
them.

[1] *H.E.* VII. 32.
[2] Eusebius does not, in his extant works, mention the
Life of Pamphilus by Pierius.

Very difficult[1] to date is the *Adversus Hieroclem*,
a work which seems to differ a great deal from the
other works of Eusebius, but which must belong
to this period. As in the case of his work *Against
Porphyry* Eusebius does not quote or mention the
Adversus Hieroclem in any of his other works. Hierocles was a Roman governor to whom persecution
was a pious duty as well as an imperial command.
When persecution broke out he was Governor of
Bithynia,[2] and later became Praefect of Egypt,
probably in A.D. 306,[3] and his anti-Christian zeal was
such that he assaulted the Christians with the pen
as well as with the sword. Whether, in the case of
Hierocles, the pen was the mightier weapon, or not,
we cannot tell, as his work is lost. Eusebius makes
it out to be a reproduction of the worn-out arguments of Celsus, and others, which Hierocles, the
'Lover of Truth', had pilfered, and for a general
refutation of Hierocles' position he refers his
readers to Origen's work.[4] But Hierocles went
further than Celsus, and had set up a parallel
between Apollonius of Tyana, and Christ. This is
the portion of the work against which the *Adversus
Hieroclem* is directed; though Eusebius states that

[1] Lightfoot (*D.C.B.*): 'Probably one of the earliest works
of Eusebius'; Harnack (*Chronologie*): 'probably before 303';
Schwartz (P.W.): 'in the year after the persecution'; etc.

[2] Lactantius, *De Mort. Pers.* XVI. 4.

[3] Norman H. Baynes in *Classical Quarterly*, 1924, vol. XVIII,
p. 190.   [4] *Adv. H.* chap. I.

the other portions of it also call for a refutation in due season, notwithstanding Origen. Porphyry, we may notice, is not mentioned as one of the sources of Hierocles, and perhaps he only formed a source of secondary importance; it was quite likely that the arguments of Celsus would be more acceptable to the energetic Roman official than the philosophy of Porphyry was. Eusebius makes merry over the inconsistencies and absurdities of the account of Apollonius, and finds that 'to love truth' in the sense in which Hierocles uses the expression implies a love of a great deal of nonsense.

It is plain that the work was written after Hierocles became Praefect of Egypt. He is twice[1] mentioned as holding supreme office, in a tone which would make one imagine that the province referred to was the one in which the writer of the refutation lived. Hierocles is in charge of 'the supreme[2] courts throughout the whole province'. There is no indication whether Hierocles was still in office or not when Eusebius wrote, and there is little indication of what was happening at the time. One passage[3] might refer to the peace of the Church, but we must remember that in a work such as this, a controversial work, the writer has to try to make

[1] *Adv. H.* 4, 19. Conybeare is of this opinion; see 'Hierocles' in the index to his translation), Loeb Library (Philostratus, *Life of Apollonius of Tyana*).
[2] *Adv. H. loc. cit.*; same expression both times.
[3] Chap. 4.

71

the body to which he belongs as important and glorious as possible. As we have seen, Eusebius was in Egypt probably before 307. Therefore he may have seen Hierocles at work, in the first year of his appointment to his new office, with all the enthusiasm which a new appointment brings. Perhaps the strong condemnation which Hierocles poured on the Christians was not only written but also verbal, and his firm and, in his own opinion, correct judgement against the Christians (κατὰ Χριστιανῶν) may be an echo of what Eusebius himself had heard.[1] We may notice that the title of the work of Hierocles was not κατὰ Χριστιανῶν[2] but πρὸς Χριστιανούς. The expression of Eusebius was therefore a reference not so much to his work as to his actual words, and the *Adversus Hieroclem* may be dated A.D. 306–7, and possibly was written in Egypt.[3]

The works of Eusebius mentioned in this and in the previous chapter were really but the foundation for his greater works, for the *Praeparatio* and *Demonstratio Evangelica*, and for the *Historia Ecclesiastica*; although these works belong, in part, to the closing period of the persecution, i.e. A.D. 311–13, they also belong to the succeeding period. It is by these longer works that the reputation of Eusebius must stand or fall, but the earlier works are important as collections of material.

[1] *Adv. H. loc. cit.*
[2] Lact. *Div. inst.* 5. 2. Lightfoot, *D.C.B. loc. cit.* p. 328.
[3] Cf. previous page, note 1.

CHAPTER IV

The Outbreak of the Arian Controversy[1]

Caesarea was, as Origen had found, a convenient home for one whose cause was lost at Alexandria, and hither about the year 321 came Arius, a presbyter of the Alexandrian Church, who had been excommunicated for heresy. The immediate cause of the trouble was simple enough, a controversy between the presbyter and his bishop on a point of Scripture, but its roots went far below the surface. It was the most serious internal conflict which the Church had yet faced; the views of Arius so commended themselves to many prominent bishops that the fabric of the Church was rent from top to bottom. Unlike the troubles with Donatists and Meletians, which were confined within the bounds of single provinces, the strife engendered by the teaching of Arius was coextensive with the existence of Christianity. It

[1] This chapter, and the two which follow it, are much indebted to the work of M. Weis, *Die Stellung des Eusebios von Cäsarea im arianischen Streit* (Trier, 1919). Reference has hardly been made to this work in the footnotes, but the bulk of the passages used in explaining the doctrinal position of Eusebius were drawn from it, and also the points of dependence and difference between the position of Eusebius and that of Origen and his successors at Alexandria. Debts to other works used are acknowledged in the notes.

would be a mistake to suppose, however, that it was the influence of the Alexandrian presbyter which bent so many bishops to his doctrines. The doctrines were there before Arius became notorious; the 'Arian' controversy is a mere name from the individual who was unfortunate enough to be implicated in the actual incidents of the outbreak; sooner or later the Church had to arrive at an accurate definition of the nature of the person whose name she bore, and for better or worse it was in this generation that the battle had to be fought.

Arius had no intention of letting his excommunication conclude the matter; he thought that he was in the right and that his bishop was in the wrong; he desired that he might return to Alexandria with his supporters, and that they should teach their own congregations in their own churches, while remaining in communion with the bishop. To secure this end Arius bestirred himself energetically, and sought, by solicitation of bishops of other countries, to put pressure on the Bishop of Alexandria. As protagonist of his cause he enlisted Eusebius of Nicomedia, who had been his fellow-pupil in the school of Lucian at Antioch, and he persuaded Eusebius of Caesarea, Paulinus of Tyre, and Patrophilus of Scythopolis to write to Alexander on his behalf. The letter[1] of Eusebius shows that

[1] Migne, *P.L.* vol. cxxix, col. 429. Mansi, *SS. Concil. Collect.* vol. xiii, p. 315.

74

he regarded Arius as misrepresented by Alexander; but the fact that Eusebius bestirred himself on Arius' behalf shows that he must have considered the presbyter as being in the right, at any rate as much as the bishop was. It was a triumph for Arius to have won the support of the Bishop of Caesarea, whose great works, the *Praeparatio* and *Demonstratio Evangelica*, in which so much bearing on the disputed questions was said, must have been already written, if not published.

We must now consider the relation of the thought of Eusebius to that of Arius and we shall see that it is very unlikely that he was influenced by Arius in one single particular: a man who had spent so much time on the study of Christian literature was not likely, at the age of about sixty years, to accept a theology, ready made, from this upstart presbyter of Alexandria. For the sake of clearness, it will be well to state the main points in the Arian teaching at the outset, then to turn to the thought of Eusebius as expressed in his works, and to deal with his relation to earlier teachers, and finally to point out the agreements and differences between Eusebius and Arius.

The teaching of Arius on the nature of the Logos may be briefly summed up as follows:

1. The Logos was created out of nothing (ἐξ οὐκ ὄντων): as a necessary consequence it follows that

2. The Logos was not begotten 'ex substantia

75

patris', but is from some lower essence (ἐξ ὑποκει-μένου τινός).

3. The Logos is begotten of the free will of the Father.

4. 'There was', though there was not a time,[1] when the Logos was not.

5. The Logos is liable to change, and only attained to unchangeableness through constant practice of the good.

When Eusebius wrote the *Praeparatio* and *Demonstratio Evangelica*, the Arian controversy, if it had broken out, had not attained to formidable proportions: the necessity for exact theological language was not therefore so insistent as it was later; but the early date of these important works is really a gain as they show us what Eusebius thought before the controversy began to put pressure on him. In studying the position of Eusebius as revealed in his works one must take account of the fact that some of his works, like the *Contra Marcellum* and the *De Ecclesiastica Theologia*, were written with polemical import almost at the close of his life, while various letters, or fragments of letters, from which some evidence can be gained, were written under the stress of the storm which Arius raised among the eastern bishops. But in another way we cannot regard the works of Eusebius as of entirely a satisfactory nature for the discernment

---

[1] Gwatkin, *Studies of Arianism*, p. 24.

of his position. In the *Demonstratio Evangelica*, for instance, one's first impression, induced by the heaping of prophecy on prophecy and of interpretation on interpretation, is that the mind of the writer was somewhat chaotic; and this is in fact the case to some extent.[1] Perhaps the ancients as well gained this impression from his works, and this fact may account, in some measure, for the extraordinary variety of opinions held with regard to the position of Eusebius by contemporaries and later writers, none of whom, we may be sure, made a systematic study of his works to try to find out what he really did think.

In considering the works of Eusebius it will be simplest to forsake chronology for once and take all together. Where the earlier and later works coincide we may be sure that the view of Eusebius did not change, but differences between them must be noted in order that the influence of the controversy on him may be perceived. Some of the differences, it must be stated, do not imply real change in the views of Eusebius, but only explicit support or condemnation of views which he had previously

---

[1] Prestige in *J. Th.S.* vol. xxiv (1923), pp. 486 ff.: ἀγέν[ν]ητος and γεν[ν]ητός, *and kindred words in Eusebius and the early Arians:* 'Eusebius really did not distinguish ἀγένητος from ἀγέννητος.' D'Alès, *Le Dogme de Nicée*, p. 111, points out that Athanasius did not distinguish explicitly between these words.

supported or rejected, though not in the terms which controversy demanded.

The chief, one might say the only, doctrinal influence which carried weight with Eusebius was the Alexandrian, and for him Alexandrian theology went back to Origen. But we must not suppose that he was indebted to Origen solely, notwithstanding his great reverence for him. After Origen came Dionysius, Theognostus and Pierius; finally he gained his knowledge of the teaching of these scholars from Pamphilus.[1] We shall see that in the points of doctrine which bear on the Arian controversy there is considerable divergence from Origen and considerable agreement with the later Alexandrians in the works of Eusebius. There is little, if anything, original in his thought: his mind was incapable of it.[2]

In various points touching the subordination of the Logos Eusebius agrees with Origen. The Logos is not ὁ πρῶτος θεός,[3] but is δεύτερος θεός.[4] Nor

[1] Though he may have known Pierius, as has already been stated.

[2] Cf. Preuschen quoted by Weis, *op. cit.* p. 17; also Eus. *De Ecclesiastica Theologia*, Preface, νεώτερον μὲν λέγειν ἔχων οὐδέν, οὐδ᾽ ἐμαυτοῦ σοφόν τι καὶ οἰκεῖον εὕρεμα.

[3] Cf. *Contra Cels.* VI. 47 with *D.E.* IV. 3 (147 d). *E.Th.* II. 17. 2.

[4] Cf. *Contra Cels.* V. 49, *Princip.* I. 3. 5, with *D.E.* IV. 7 (156 c): δευτέρως ἡμῖν μετὰ τὸν τῶν ὅλων θεὸν κυριολογούμενον. *D.E.* IV. 3 (147 d).

78

is the Logos ὁ τῶν ὅλων θεός or ὁ ἐπὶ πᾶσι[1] (πάντων (Eus.)) θεός. A more important fact is the denial to the Son of the title ἀληθινὸς θεός[2] or ὁ θεός[3] (i.e. He is θεός without the article, as in St John i. 1, καὶ θεὸς ἦν ὁ λόγος). Eusebius always held this view both before[3] and during[4],[5] the controversy, and he bases his view on Scripture (St John xvii. 3). In Origen the Son is not αὐταγαθός,[6] nor ὡς ἁπλῶς ἀγαθός, nor ἀγαθὸς ἀπαραλλάκτως,[6] while in Eusebius the Father is μόνον ἀληθῶς ἀγαθός:[7] the Son, in both Origen and Eusebius,[8] has not the same worship as the Father. Eusebius does recognise the difficulty raised on this last point in St John v. 23 (ἵνα πάντες τιμῶσι τὸν υἱόν, καθὼς τιμῶσι τὸν πάτερα) and states that this refers to worship that is almost the same (παραπλησίως).[9] The Son Himself honoured the Father and therefore the Father

[1] De Orat. 15. In Joh. ii. 3. Eus. uses these expressions constantly and only uses them of the Father.
[2] In Joh. ii. 3. Cf. P.E. vii. 15 (327 d).
[3] In Joh. ii. 2. Cf. D.E. v. 4 (226 c).
[4] Migne, P.L. vol. cxxix, col. 430. Mansi, SS. Concil. Collect. vol. xiii, p. 317: καὶ αὐτὸς μὲν θεὸς ὁ λόγος, ἀλλ᾽ οὐκ ἀληθινὸς θεός. Athanasius, De Synodis, 17, notices this point with regard to Eusebius. He notes that in a letter to Euphration the bishop, written before the Council of Nicaea, Eusebius wrote that Christ was not true God.
[5] E.Th. ii. 22. 1, ii. 23. 2.
[6] Princip. i. 2. 13.   [7] D.E. v. 1 (216 b).
[8] Contra Cels. viii. 13. E.Th. ii. 7. 5
[9] E.Th. ii. 7. 14.

79

requires higher honour than the Son, who declares that He is completely dependent on the Father's will.[1]

It may be well to state here the grounds on which Eusebius recognises the divinity of the Son.

1. He is creator of all things—as in St John i.[2]

2. He is the image ($\epsilon i \kappa \acute{\omega} \nu$) of the Father, and as such He is constituted similarly to the Father.[3] As a development of the conception that the Son is the image of the Father, Eusebius[4] uses the simile of the Emperor and the statue of the Emperor.[5] Eusebius is constantly stressing[6] the likeness of the

---

[1] *E.Th.* II. 7. 5, 6. It does not seem necessary to discuss the use by Eusebius of the word $a\dot{v}\tau o\theta\epsilon\acute{o}s$ with regard to the Son, as Schwartz reads $a\dot{v}\tau\grave{o}v$ $\theta\epsilon\acute{o}v$ (with the majority of the MSS) in the passage concerned (*H.E.* X. 4. 16). This reading appears more in conformity with what we should expect from Eusebius. Origen uses $a\dot{v}\tau o\theta\epsilon\acute{o}s$ of the Father only. (*In Joh. ii.* 2.) Eusebius uses $a\dot{v}\tau\grave{o}s$ $\theta\epsilon\acute{o}s$ of the Son, *E.Th.* II. 14. 7, and in his letter to Alexander (note 4 of the previous page).

[2] *D.E.* IV. 3 (150 a); cf. *E.Th.* II. 7. 12.

[3] *D.E.* IV. 2 (146 b); *D.E.* IV. 3 (148 a); *E.Th.* I. 1. 4, etc.

[4] See Radford, *Three Teachers of Alexandria*, p. 54.

[5] *D.E.* V. 4 (226 d); *E.Th.* II. 23. 3.

[6] In particular note the following phrases:

(a) $\dot{a}\phi o\mu o\iota\hat{\omega}\sigma\theta a\iota$ $\kappa a\tau\grave{a}$ $\pi\acute{a}\nu\tau a$ (*D.E.* IV. 3 (148 a, c); *E.Th.* II. 14. 21 and III. 21. 1).

(b) $\pi a\rho o\mu o\iota\hat{\omega}\sigma\theta a\iota$ $\kappa a\tau\grave{a}$ $\pi\acute{a}\nu\tau a$, *D.E.* V. 4 (227 b).

(c) $\dot{o}\mu o\iota\acute{o}\tau a\tau o s$ $\kappa a\tau\grave{a}$ $\pi\acute{a}\nu\tau a$, *E.Th.* II. 14. 7.

The last phrase is used by Athanasius, *De Decretis Syn. Nic.* 20.

Son to the Father and from this conception he never swerved during his whole life.

When we come to consider the issues that were important in the Arian controversy, serious divergences between Origen and Eusebius are immediately apparent. On the question of the 'generatio' of the Son, for instance, they do not coincide. Origen[1] defines the Father as τὸ ἀγένητον τῶν ὅλων αἴτιον. In so far as the Son is God, the same definition suits Him, in so far as He is Son He is an αἰτιατόν, and therefore is not in the fullest sense αἴτιον τῶν ὅλων and is, therefore, not ὁ πρῶτος θεός. The Son is to be regarded as αἰτιατὸν ἀγένητον, and the 'generatio' is an eternal process, without beginning. If we deny eternity to the 'generatio' we deny the power or will of God.[2] There never was a time when God was not the Father[3] or when the Son did not exist.[4] The Logos is ἀγένητος and ἀΐδιος.[5] The unchangeable character of God postulates an eternal 'generatio', not an act begun and ended.[6] The 'generatio' is a necessary internal process.[7]

Eusebius does not follow Origen on one of these points—in fact he is generally in flat contradiction

[1] In Joh. ii. 2.　　　　　[2] Princip. I. 2. 2.
[3] Princip. loc. cit.　　　　[4] Princip. IV. 4. 1 (28).
[5] Frag. In Joh. i. 4; frag. In Joh. i. 1. Contra Cels. VI. 17.
[6] Hom. in Jer. ix. 4.
[7] See Bethune-Baker, Introduction to the Early History of Christian Doctrine, 2nd ed. p. 148, on Origen's statement that the Son is begotten of or by the will of the Father.

to him. Eusebius regards the 'generatio' not as an
eternal process, but as an act, begun and ended:
an act not in time but in a pre-temporal state:[1] he
uses the past tense with regard to it. ἀγεννησία[2] is
the peculiar quality of the Father and of the Father
alone. For Eusebius the Son is not ἀγέννητος[3] or
ἀΐδιος, which for him are synonyms, or ἄναρχος,[4] and
he actually denies these titles to the Son. He regards
the Son as begotten from the free will of the Father;
this is shown by his rejection of the much-used
metaphor of light and its ray, as a picture of the true
relations of Father and Son. The ray[5] exists as a
necessary accompaniment of the light, but the Son
is of the will of the Father (who is of course the
same after, as well as before the 'generatio').

Origen regards the Son as being of the essence
of the Father.[6] He uses the word ὁμοούσιος and
the phrase ἐκ τῆς οὐσίας τοῦ Πατρός[7] to describe
the relation. Eusebius regards the Son as from the
essence of the Father but he does not use the word

[1] Eus. *Epist. ad Alexand.*, Migne, *P.L.* vol. cxxix, col. 429.
D.E. iv. 3 (147 d). *E.Th.* i. 8. 3.
[2] ἀγεννησία Dindorf, ἀγενησία Gifford. *P.E.* vii. 19 (333 d).
The passage is a quotation from Dionysius of Alexandria
but Eusebius approves of it.
[3] *E.Th.* ii. 12. 2; cf. *D.E.* iv. 3 (148 a).
[4] *E.Th.* i. 11. 1.   [5] *D.E.* iv. 3. 8 (148 a).
[6] See frag. in Harnack, *History of Dogma*, Eng. transl. ii.
354.
[7] Frag. *In Joh. i.* 14.

ὁμοούσιος or ἐκ τῆς οὐσίας τοῦ Πατρός,[1] which are
the logical ways of describing the relationship,
once 'generatio ex substantia' has been admitted.
Of the 'generatio' of the Logos Eusebius uses the
words φύειν,[2] προβάλλειν,[3] ἀποτίκτειν,[4] γεννᾶν,[5]
and when he uses the passive of those words he uses
the preposition ἐκ, and not ὑπό, as the Arians did.[6]
The Son is produced 'from' the Father; Eusebius
also rejects the use of κτίζειν[7] to explain the
generation of the Son, and points out that κτίζειν
does signify creation, but not creation such as
implies a sharing of nature with the creator. In
this point he differs from Origen.[8] Eusebius wishes
the word κτίζειν in the crucial verse[9] of the Book
of Proverbs to mean κατατάττειν[10] or καθιστάναι—
the Son was established by the Father to rule His

[1] The words ἐκ τῆς οὐσίας τοῦ Πατρός do occur in D.E.
IV. 3 (149 a), in the following context: λόγον τε καὶ θεὸν ἐκ
θεοῦ, οὐ κατὰ διάστασιν ἢ τομὴν ἢ διαίρεσιν ἐκ τῆς τοῦ
Πατρὸς οὐσίας προβεβλημένον.
[2] E.Th. II. 14. 7.   [3] D.E. v. 1 (213 a). E.Th. I. 8. 3.
[4] E.Th. I. 10. 1.   [5] Passim.
[6] Cf. Epist. Euseb. Nic. ad Paulinum (Theodoret, H.E.
I. 5), where ὑπ᾽ αὐτοῦ, and ἐκ τῆς οὐσίας are contrasted.
[7] E.Th. I. 10. 1: κτίζει μὲν οὖν βασιλεὺς πόλιν, ἀλλ᾽ οὐ
γεννᾷ πόλιν. But it must be noted that we must go to
the E.Th. for explicit condemnation of κτίσμα; cf. note 5
on page 85.
[8] But cf. Bethune-Baker, op. cit. p. 148, note 2: 'Justinian
is the only authority for the assertion that Origen used
κτίσμα. Origen certainly never meant it in any Arian sense'.
[9] Prov. viii. 22.   [10] E.Th. III. 2. 8.

6-2

works—and he argues for this point of view at considerable length.[1] It is to be noted that we have to go to the *De Ecclesiastica Theologia* for explicit views on the meaning of κτίζειν—but the silence of his earlier works on this point does not imply sympathy with the Arian position. The Son proceeds from the Father as a beam from[2] light, as a stream from its[3] source and as a pleasant odour[4] from its source. It is quite plain that Eusebius rejected the idea that the Son was produced from nothing: he stigmatises this doctrine as οὐκ ἀκίνδυνον in the *Demonstratio Evangelica*:[5] but for explicit condemnation of it one must turn to the *De Ecclesiastica Theologia*.[6]

Before leaving this subject it must be noted that Eusebius, while regarding the Son as of the essence of the Father, does in one passage[7] at any rate distinguish the οὐσία of the Son from that of the Father. οὐσία in the passage concerned must mean 'particular or individual existence'. Origen uses[8] the word in the same sense; this usage serves to distinguish the two divine persons, and avoids Sabellianism.

---

[1] *E.Th.* III. 2. 8 ff.
[2] Eusebius uses this simile but qualifies it. See p. 82.
[3] *E.Th.* I. 2.   [4] *D.E.* IV. 3 (148 c).
[5] *D.E.* V. 1 (214 b).   [6] *E.Th.* I. 10. 4.
[7] *P.E.* VII. 15 (325 b).
[8] Bethune-Baker, *op. cit.* p. 149, note 3. Origen, *De Oratione*, 15.

84

With regard to the last of the points of Arian teaching mentioned above, the mutability of the Son, Eusebius agrees with Origen. Both are opposed to the Arian position. Origen insists[1] on the immutability of the Logos even when He accommodated Himself to the limitations of human life.[2] Eusebius never speaks of change in the Logos, and does, in fact, acknowledge unchangeableness from the 'generatio' onwards both directly and indirectly. At the 'generatio' the Father from whom all the qualities[3] of the Logos come granted unchangeableness to Him. The Son is τέλειος:[4] He is the image of the Father and He has divine life similarly with the Father. Eusebius acknowledges the unchangeability directly where he says[5] that the Logos underwent no change at the incarnation.

The three main points on which Eusebius differs from Origen are therefore:

1. The eternal existence of the Logos.
2. The necessity of the 'generatio' of the Logos.
3. The use of ὁμοούσιος.

On whom was he dependent for these variations,

---

[1] *Contra Cels.* IV. 14.
[2] The words of this sentence are borrowed from Radford, *op. cit.* p. 27.
[3] *D.E.* v. 4 (227 b, c).
[4] *D.E.* IV. 3 (147 b).
[5] *D.E.* IV. 13 (169 b). Cf. Letter of Eusebius in Mansi, *op. cit.* vol. XIII, p. 315: υἱὸν...ἄτρεπτον καὶ ἀναλλοίωτον, κτίσμα τοῦ Θεοῦ τέλειον, ἀλλ' οὐχ ὡς ἓν τῶν κτισμάτων.

85

all of which show a tendency toward Arian teaching? Did he first give voice to them when the Arian controversy became the most important feature of the history of the Church? In his letter to Alexander in support of Arius, written at the beginning of the controversy, Eusebius states that he is on the side of those who believed that the 'generatio' of the Logos was not without beginning and finds it extraordinary that anyone could have believed otherwise. It is unlikely that Eusebius got this view from Arius: where he did get it, and also his objection to ὁμοούσιος, was in the post-Origen Alexandrians Dionysius and Theognostus, in whose teaching opposition to Sabellianism was the main point.

Dionysius, for instance, was reproved by his namesake of Rome for not using ὁμοούσιος, but excused himself on the ground that the word was not used in Scripture.[1] He denied the eternity of the Logos (καὶ γὰρ ὡς ποίημα ὤν, οὐκ ἦν πρὶν γένη-ται)[2] but believed in the 'generatio ex substantia', as is shown by the metaphors that he uses of parents and children, and source and stream.[3] Thus we find these Eusebian beliefs in Dionysius, and also again

[1] Ath. *De Sent. Dion.* 18.

[2] Ath. *op. cit.* 4.

[3] Dionysius also said that the Son was ξένος κατ' οὐσίαν in His relation to the Father, but this is merely a means of emphasising the distinct existence of Father and Son. Ath. *op. cit.* 18.

86

in Theognostus who believed in 'generatio ex substantia' and who uses the phrase ἐκ τῆς οὐσίας τοῦ Πατρός, which, in his mind, implies only ὁμοιότης[1] between Father and Son. This is a very important point when we realise the insistence of Eusebius on the likeness between the two divine persons. We may also compare the use of the word κανών by Theognostus[2]—'God wishing to create the Universe first produced the Son like some κανών of creation'—with a similar usage in Eusebius, 'in order that all things might be made straight by him...as through one all wise and living instrument, and a skilful and intelligent rule'.[3] Eusebius does not mention this teacher in the *Church History*, and perhaps his debt to him is exaggerated by the fact that we know of these Alexandrian beliefs only through the fragments of the authors concerned. We cannot be certain of assigning particular doctrines to particular teachers when the writings of these teachers are extant only in fragments.

We have thus seen that Eusebius was dependent on these Alexandrians for two of the three main points on which he differed from Origen. Is it not

---

[1] See Radford, *op. cit.* p. 26. The ὁμοιότης of Theognostus is πλήρης and ἀκριβής. Theognostus also spoke of the οὐσία of the Son.

[2] Frag. in Gregory of Nyssa, *Contra Eunom.* 3.

[3] Eus. *D.E.* IV. 2 (146 c).

therefore more probable that he was dependent on some one or other of them for his third deviation from Origen, i.e. that the Son is 'of the will' of the Father, rather than on Arius?

Once speculation had proceeded so far as these thinkers carried it, Arianism followed almost of necessity.[1] Eusebius added nothing to the doctrines of those who had gone before. He agrees with Arius on two of the five points set forth above, (1) that the Son was begotten of the free will of the Father, and (2) that 'there was', though there was not a time, when the Son was not. On one point he had expressed no very definite condemnation of Arian teaching, i.e. it was only οὐκ ἀκίνδυνον to suggest that the Son was created from nothing, and on two points he is against Arius. (1) Eusebius believed that the Logos was produced 'ex substantia patris' as against the very definite view set forth by his namesake of Nicomedia:[2] 'But there is one unbegotten, and one begotten by him truly and not from his essence, having no share at all in the nature of the unbegotten, nor his existence from his essence'. (2) With regard to the Arian teaching that the Logos is not unchangeable by nature, but has attained to unchangeableness through constant practice of the good, Eusebius is at variance with

[1] Though Arius himself, and Eusebius of Nicomedia, were products of the school of Lucian of Antioch.
[2] Epist. Eus. Nic. ad Paulinum (Theodoret, *H.E.* I. 5).

Arius and his followers who did not differentiate between the Logos and other creatures, nor make His excellence greater than that of any virtuous man.[1]

Thus, at the outbreak of the controversy, Eusebius occupied a middle position: a position lying near enough to Arianism to give Arius encouragement. Eusebius was in some ways an open-minded man; in the *Demonstratio Evangelica* he lays down no hard and fast fulfilments of prophecies which all should accept; often he gives various interpretations and leaves his readers to make their choice; this open-mindedness may have followed him into the realm of dogma: Arius should have justice: let Alexander receive him back just as Demetrius had received back the Alexandrian delinquent of the previous century, influenced, perhaps, by a letter to which the Bishop of Caesarea of that time was one of the chief signatories.

It may not be out of place to add here a few words concerning the teaching of Eusebius on the Holy Ghost, although this was not one of the crucial points of the controversy in its early stages. The Holy Ghost belongs to the Holy Trinity[2] but is only the greatest of the creatures made by the Son to whom He is inferior.[3] The Holy Ghost was

[1] Alexander in Theodoret, I. 4.
[2] *P.E.* XI. 20.
[3] *P.E.* VII. 15 (541 b ff.).

produced μὴ ἐκ τοῦ Πατρὸς ὁμοίως τῷ Υἱῷ[1] but is a creation of the Son, because 'all things were made by Him'. The Son alone is sharer in the power,[2] essence,[2] and dominion[3] of the Father. The sphere of action of the Holy Spirit is less wide than that of the Father and Son[4]—the Spirit is restricted μόνοις ἁγίοις. In his conceptions Eusebius differs from Origen, chiefly on the questions of the Divinity[5] and Eternity[6] of the Holy Ghost. He degrades the Holy Spirit and probably got his views from Theognostus and Pierius, who, according to Photius,[7] taught heretically about the third person of the Holy Trinity.

---

[1] *E. Th.* III. 6. 3. 'Subordinationism in its most outspoken boldness', Swete, *The Holy Spirit in the Ancient Church*, p. 197.
[2] *D.E.* IV. 6 (155 a).   [3] *D.E.* V. 3 (220 d).
[4] *E. Th.* III. 6. 1.
[5] *Princip.* I. 3. 7.   [6] *Princip.* I. 3. 4.
[7] *Cod.* 106, 119. Cf. Radford, *op. cit.* p. 52. Photius says of Pierius: ὑποβεβηκέναι γὰρ αὐτὸ (i.e. τὸ Πνεῦμα) τῆς τοῦ Πατρὸς καὶ τοῦ Υἱοῦ ἀποφάσκει δόξης.

CHAPTER V

Nicaea

But as the theological struggle deepened, events were taking place which were to have a decisive effect on the Church in general, and on the controversy in particular. In 323 Constantine became master of the whole Roman Empire, and the removal of Licinius, whose anti-Christian bias had become more and more pronounced, left the field clear for the intervention of an emperor who had always shown himself friendly to the Church and to whose policy a united Church in a united Empire was a necessity. He already had had full experience of the nature of Christian controversy in Africa; the general temper of controversy in Egypt, whether secular or religious, must have been known to him: what Constantine wanted was peace.

In the first instance, he was willing to let the Church itself settle the dispute, which seemed to him a matter of words, a stupid attempt to ascertain the unascertainable. The letter which he addressed to the disputants is a curious document, in the authenticity of which it is a little hard to believe.[1] Its general tone, however, is probably a correct

[1] *V.C.* II 64 ff. Batiffol in *Bulletin d'ancienne littérature et d'archéologie chrétiennes*, April 15th, 1914.

reflection of the attitude of the Emperor. Hosius, Bishop of Corduba, went to the East as emissary of Constantine, but by this time the dispute was past cure by the simple means of reconciliation, and it had attained to such proportions that no local Synod could restore peace. A General Synod of at any rate the Church of the Eastern half of the Empire was necessary, and Constantine called one to meet at Ancyra towards the end of A.D. 324. But before this Synod met the Arian party received a severe blow. At a Synod in Antioch, called, no doubt, to elect a successor to Bishop Philogonius, a creed was formulated, approximating to that of Alexander, and three bishops, who refused to sign, were provisionally excommunicated: these three were Theodotus of Laodicea, Narcissus of Neronias in Cilicia, and Eusebius of Caesarea.[1] Their case was to come up at the General Synod of Ancyra.

Now it is plain that Eusebius had been somewhat

---

[1] Schwartz in P.W. *loc. cit.* col. 1411. Cf. the supposed reference to this by Alexander in Theodoret, I. 3, οὐκ οἶδ' ὅπως ἐν Συρίᾳ χειροτονηθέντες ἐπίσκοποι τρεῖς. The whole question of this Synod of Antioch is a very complicated one, and has not been entered into in the present work. There is a short and clear statement of the situation in A. E. Burn, *The Council of Nicaea*, pp. 12–19: on p. 15 he writes: 'if it (the condemnation) can be finally accepted as true history, it clears up a good deal that was very hazy in our accounts of the situation'.

indiscreet in his support of Arius—he had been
far more active than Paulinus of Tyre had been,
though, doctrinally speaking, Paulinus stood far
nearer to Arius than Eusebius did. Eusebius of
Nicomedia, writing[1] to Paulinus, reproves him for
his silence but praises the zeal of Eusebius of
Caesarea for the Arian cause. This probably refers
to the excommunication of Eusebius at this Synod.
Arius also places Eusebius first in a list of his supporters, who, he says, had been condemned for
saying that God had an existence prior to that of
his Son.[2]

The Synod of Antioch was a triumph for the
extremists—no doubt they had carefully laid their
plans to get in this first blow. Constantine was
alarmed—he saw that peace was impossible if this
sort of thing went on unchecked—the Synod of
Ancyra would be held in another extremist strong-
hold—the Bishop of that see, Marcellus, was a
most uncompromising opponent of Arius. Therefore Constantine made an attempt to raise the
Great Synod out of an atmosphere of party by
changing its place of meeting to Nicaea in Bithynia,
where it would be conveniently under the shadow
of the imperial court. We cannot suppose that the
good climate[3] of Nicaea alleged by Constantine

[1] Theodoret, *H.E.* I. 6.
[2] Theodoret, *H.E.* I. 5.
[3] Cowper, *Syriac Miscellanies*, pp. I, 6.

93

was the real reason[1] for the transference of the Council from Ancyra.

Eusebius and his friend Paulinus of Tyre passed through Ancyra on their way to Nicaea. Marcellus was not at home[2] when they were in his city, but both the travellers seem to have been outspoken in his absence, and Marcellus declares that Eusebius said that there were two divine essences, while Paulinus said, among other things, that Christ was a second God. But we must remember that Marcellus was writing some time after the event, and had not himself heard the words which the two friends were alleged to have uttered. As far as Eusebius is concerned the words which Marcellus attributes to him are not in contradiction to statements[3] in his written works, though it is going too far to attribute heresy to Eusebius because he laid great emphasis on the division of the two divine persons, while recognising that the Son proceeded from the essence of the Father: the time, too, would

---

[1] Cf. Norman H. Baynes in *J.Th.S.* vol. XXVI, p. 42, for a somewhat similar ruse used by Constantine in dealing with the Donatists.

[2] Cf. *C.M.* I. 4. 45, ἅπερ φησὶν ἐξ ἀκοῆς μεμαθηκέναι. Zahn, *Marcellus von Ancyra*, p. 43, note 4, regards the Eusebius who preached at Ancyra as Eusebius of Nicomedia. Lightfoot supports this view in *D.C.B. loc. cit.*, but Klostermann in the introduction (p. xiv) to his edition of the *C.M.* and *E.Th.* takes the view that it was our Eusebius. Schwartz, in P.W. *loc. cit.* col. 1411, also takes this latter view.

[3] *P.E.* VII. 15 (325 b).

be singularly inappropriate for such a display of heresy on Eusebius' part.

The assembly at Nicaea was the most wonderful and impressive spectacle which had ever been seen in the history of the Church, and no circumstance of temporal splendour was omitted by the Emperor to impress his new allies with a due sense of his power. Eusebius has preserved for us a glowing description[1] of the opening of the Council—'we cannot wonder if the old historian turned away from the noisy bickerings of after years to recall the glorious hope which gathered round the Council's meeting'.[2]

A certain bishop delivered the opening address to the Emperor after he had taken his seat. In the *Vita Constantini*[3] Eusebius describes the speaker as τῶν ἐπισκόπων ὁ τοῦ δεξιοῦ τάγματος πρωτεύων. Who is this person? Eusebius himself, or some other? The ancient authors are very much divided on the subject. Eustathius[4] of Antioch, Alexander of Alexandria,[5] and Eusebius[6] of Caesarea are all given. In view of this diversity of opinion the 'silence of Eusebius' in the *Vita Constantini* is very tantalising. His method of mentioning the speech is much the same as that with which he introduces

[1] *V.C.* III. 10.   [2] Gwatkin, *op. cit.* p. 36.
[3] *V.C.* III. 11.   [4] Theod. *H.E.* I. 6.
[5] According to Nicetas Choniates (*Thes. de Orth. Fid.* v. 7), who bases his statement on Theodore of Mopsuestia and Philostorgius.   [6] Sozomen, *H.E.* I. 19.

95

his sermon at Tyre in the tenth book of the *Historia Ecclesiastica*, and he himself[1] says that he delivered a laudatory oration on the Vicennalia of Constantine in the midst of an assembly of God's ministers. But an oration in praise of the victorious[2] Emperor at his Vicennalia[3] is not the same as an inaugural oration at the meeting of a Church Council. Eusebius always wishes to make the most of his acquaintance with the Emperor, and it is surprising that he passes over his own speech on so important an occasion with so little notice. Moreover, there is no reason whatever why Eusebius should have been singled out for this honour, learned man though he was: he was not a bishop of one of the greatest sees, he had already been indiscreet in his support of Arius, and in his outspoken preaching at Ancyra: his personal acquaintance with Constantine was not yet begun: he arrived at the Council with the stigma of condemnation by a local Synod on him. At the moment he was hardly a fit person to perform this function. The heading of the chapter[4] of the *Vita Constantini* in question is 'Silence of the Synod after a short speech[5] by Eusebius the Bishop'. But of what see was Eusebius the bishop? Caesarea, or

---

[1] *V.C.* I. I.   [2] τὸν καλλίνικον.

[3] See Westcott, *The Two Empires*, p. 323, who thinks that the oration of Eusebius was at the Vicennalia.

[4] *V.C.* III. II.   [5] μετὰ τὸ εἰπεῖν τι.

Nicomedia? The chapter heading seems the source from which Sozomen drew his information that Eusebius of Caesarea was the bishop in question. Now the metropolitan of the province of Bithynia, in which the Synod was being held, was Eusebius of Nicomedia. It seems likely that he should be selected to deliver the oration.[1] Besides being the local metropolitan, he was an influential man at court. If he was not to deliver the speech we must fall back on the bishop of one of the great sees, and not on Eusebius of Caesarea.[2]

In pursuance of the Emperor's peaceful policy no efforts were spared to reach a solution, which, while embracing the whole Church except utter irreconcilables, would provide a suitable creed for the bishops to sign as a test[3] of orthodoxy. We have no coherent account of the Council's proceedings, but the struggle over the faith was long and bitter.[4] At some stage in the proceedings Eusebius read his Caesarean creed. It is generally supposed that his introduction of the creed of his own Church was an attempt by Eusebius to evolve a compromise between the opposing parties. But is it not more likely that at its first presentation he

[1] Schwartz in P.W. *loc. cit.* col. 1413.
[2] 'Harnack may be right in suggesting that the occupants of the great sees may have presided in turn', Burn, *op. cit.* p. 28.
[3] Cf. Gwatkin, *op. cit.* p. 37.
[4] Eus. *V.C.* III. 13.

read his Caesarean creed as a proof[1] of his orthodoxy in order to obtain a rehabilitation, in view of
his condemnation at the Synod of Antioch? The
letter[2] which he addressed to his own Church after
the Council appears to confirm this view. In this
letter, 'the faith put forward by us' is not a creed
by itself, but a creed plus a declaration by Eusebius
that this had always been the teaching of his
Church, that he himself had always held it—calling
to witness God the Almighty and the Lord Jesus
Christ—that he can produce evidence, and per-
suade the assembly by proof that he had always
believed and preached this faith. This personal
emphasis on what he himself had done is surely a
reference to his own case. If he was proposing the
Caesarean creed as a rule of faith for the use of the
whole Church there was no need for all these
references to himself. The creed of Caesarea first
made its appearance in that august assembly as
evidence for the orthodoxy of Eusebius, not as a
proposed creed for the whole of Christendom.

When the creed had been set forth, says Eusebius, there was no room to gainsay it. He was
rehabilitated. The Emperor himself was the first
to testify to its orthodoxy—Constantine's judgement carried great weight, though theologically
speaking it was practically worthless. Now the

[1] Schwartz in P.W. *loc. cit.* col. 1412. Burn, *op. cit.* p. 31.
[2] Theodoret, *H.E.* I. 12.

emergence of the Caesarean creed was able to move the discussion an important stage forward. Up to the moment no progress had been made, though possibly Arian hopes had already been destroyed by the rejection of a creed presented by Eusebius of Nicomedia. That at best was a negative result. The Caesarean creed was a basis on which all were agreed, and formed a convenient starting-point for the formulation of the document which was to embrace the faith of the whole Church. It was impossible that the creed should be accepted as it stood: Alexandria and Antioch would be most unwilling to allow their own local creeds to be put aside for the Caesarean, which in itself appeared to afford no safeguard against Arianism.

The Emperor, prompted perhaps by Hosius, suggested the addition to the creed of the word ὁμοούσιος, as an explanation of the relation of the Son to the Father. But things were not left there, and Eusebius received back his creed in a form to which he could not subscribe without question of the terms involved. In an aggrieved tone Eusebius writes, 'Our wisest and most religious emperor reasoned thus, but they' (whoever 'they' may be) 'on the excuse of the addition of ὁμοούσιος have produced the following document'. We must now consider in what way the Eusebian Logos differs from the Logos of the Nicene Creed, according to which the Logos is γεννηθέντα ἐκ τοῦ Πατρὸς μονογενῆ, τουτέστιν ἐκ τῆς οὐσίας τοῦ Πατρός, Θεὸν ἐκ Θεοῦ, καὶ φῶς ἐκ φωτός, Θεὸν ἀληθινὸν ἐκ Θεοῦ ἀληθινοῦ, γεννηθέντα οὐ ποιηθέντα, ὁμοούσιον τῷ Πατρί.

Eusebius[1] here came up against several conceptions to which he did not, previous to the Council, assent: he had to give an explanation to his flock at Caesarea of why he assented to these conceptions, and why these were accepted in preference to their own local creed: we must now consider the Eusebian interpretation of the doubtful expressions.

The first of these was the meaning of ἐκ τῆς οὐσίας τοῦ Πατρός, to which is joined the word ὁμοούσιος. To explain this Eusebius merely harks back to his Caesarean creed and explains it as meaning that the Son is from the Father and that the generation of the Son does not imply any division, modification or alteration of the divine essence, that the Son of God does not resemble in any one respect the creatures that He has made, but to the Father alone, who begat Him, He is in all points alike (κατὰ πάντα τρόπον ὅμοιον). This, we may note, is not the explanation given by Athanasius, who states that resemblance is not sufficient but that the Son is ταὐτὸν τῇ ὁμοιώσει ἐκ τοῦ Πατρός.[2] Moreover, Eusebius knew that the

[1] See Gwatkin, *op. cit.* p. 46.
[2] *De Decr. Syn. Nic.* 20.

expression ὁμοούσιος had been used by certain
distinguished bishops and writers of the past to
describe the divinity of the Father and the Son,
and therefore it seemed right to accept it. The
expression 'begotten not made' is accepted because
this expression served to differentiate the Son from
all things that were created by Him, to which He is
in no respect similar.

At the end of the creed were anathemas directed
against Arianism specifically, against those who
said (1) ἦν ποτὲ ὅτε οὐκ ἦν, (2) πρὶν γεννηθῆναι
οὐκ ἦν, (3) ὅτι ἐξ οὐκ ὄντων ἐγένετο. Eusebius
makes a somewhat lame excuse for signing these
anathemas, which, he knew, involved condemnation of the beliefs of many of his friends and of his
own beliefs in part. As his reason for signing he
gives for anathemas (1) and (3) the fact that the
expressions concerned were not scriptural,[1] and
that he had never used the expressions himself.
There is not a word to show that they were an
explicit condemnation of Arian doctrine. On the
second anathema he makes a yet more amazing
statement, 'the condemnation of the assertion that
"before he was begotten he was not" did not
appear to involve any incongruity, because all assent
to the fact that He was the Son of God before He

[1] Cf. Leclercq, op. cit. col. 754: 'Il n'imaginait un bon
symbole, qu'en parfilant des lambeaux et des mots détachés
de l'Écriture Sainte'. Yet he let ὁμοούσιος pass.

was begotten according to the flesh'.[1] The Arians, however, admitted that the Son had existed previous to the incarnation. The statement of Eusebius means nothing. Athanasius[2] refers to this very passage, and says that Eusebius in this passage made the accusation against the Arians that they did not believe in the existence of the Son previous to His birth in the flesh. But the difficulty is that this[3] was an Arian belief. Eusebius has recourse to a quibble: as we have seen he believed in the generation of the Logos as a pre-temporal act, and where his own belief is concerned he interprets the anathema in his own way. Finally he explains away the anathema by stating that the Son existed potentially in the Father before he was begotten. The adoption of the new creed did not cause Eusebius to give up one jot or tittle of his own beliefs: an expression like ὁμοούσιος he ignored, and in his later works he never stands forth as a defender of the 'Nicene' faith.

Eusebius signed. Can it be said that there was any honesty in his act, or did he sign in dissimulation as some of the straightforward Arians did?[4]

[1] Translated by Gwatkin, *Selections from Early Christian Writers*, p. 185.   [2] *De Decr. Syn. Nic.* 3.
[3] I.e. The existence of the Son previous to His birth in the flesh.
[4] Philostorgius, *H.E.* 1. 9 (p. 10, Bidez). He includes Eusebius among the Ἀρειόφρονες (p. 9, l. 15, Bidez). Cf. Theodoret, 1. 7.

His resistance, it may be inferred, was tenacious for one day, and his signing was a surprise to Athanasius.[1] The expressions concerned must have seemed to him to involve a sacrifice, both of himself and of his friends. He was considered two-faced by some because of his 'desertion' of the Arians,[2] who must have expected his support after his actions previous to the Council. The influence which was the most powerful in affecting the decision of Eusebius was that of the Emperor. What the Emperor wanted was that as many as possible should be embraced within the circle of the Catholic Church, though even Constantine must have known that some irreconcilables would always stand out. Eusebius[3] is emphatic that the reconciliation of Nicaea was due to Constantine. Peace was so precious[4] that it must be attained even at the cost of mental reservations. Constantine wished the creed to be accepted, and that each should put his own interpretation on it. In Eusebius' letter we have a specimen of one type of interpretation. The actions of Eusebius at the Council were a puzzle to his contemporaries and to succeeding generations: and, as in the case of the creed, each put his own interpretation on them. Of the two

[1] *De Decr. Syn. Nic.* 3, παράδοξον.
[2] Socrates, *H.E.* I. 23.   [3] *V.C.* III. 13.
[4] Cf. the letter of Eusebius: τοῦ τῆς εἰρήνης σκοποῦ πρὸ ὀφθαλμῶν κειμένου.

writers who stand nearest to him, Athanasius never shows bitterness against Eusebius and does not pillory him as an Arian, though he had good reason to attack him, while Hilary of Poitiers enumerates him among the Arian band. Jerome denounces him as a complete Arian, but he is not an honest witness as the Origen controversy coloured his views. In his *De Viris Illustribus*,[1] written before the outbreak of that controversy, he lets the fact that Eusebius wrote a defence of Origen pass without censure. Socrates is out to defend the orthodoxy of the Father of Church history and is guilty of various suppressions[2] which make his witness as suspect as that of Jerome. Nor does Sozomen doubt his orthodoxy, while Theodoret regarded Eusebius as an Arian. Philostorgius, himself an Arian, wished to show that the most learned man in the Nicene Council was a partisan of Arius, while Gelasius of Cyzicus is determined to

[1] 81.

[2] In particular:

I. He makes out (*H.E.* I. 8) that Eusebius' delay in signing was of little importance, whereas Eusebius himself makes it very important.

II. He omits the passage in which Eusebius excuses himself for signing anathema (2) *supra*—a passage preserved by Theodoret.

III. He does not mention the letters of Arius to Eusebius of Nicomedia, and of Eusebius of Nicomedia to Paulinus of Tyre.

IV. He does not show the prominent part taken by Eusebius in the attack on Athanasius in the years following the Council of Nicaea.

show how completely orthodox Eusebius was. Here
we may mention, in passing, the fact that Gelasius
adduces sources, such as the proceedings of the
Council, which no one else seems to have used, and
he makes Eusebius the protagonist in the refutation
of the Arian philosopher Phaedo, a refutation in
which the Bishop of Caesarea uses of the Son
expressions such as ὁμότιμος τῷ Πατρί, ἀληθινὸς
Θεός, ἄναρχος, ἀίδιος, ὁμοούσιος, which he hated,
and is thrust forward to defend the Nicene faith,
which he had so strenuously opposed. Epiphanius
regards Eusebius as at any rate a supporter of
Arius, and Antipater of Bostra regarded him as a
heretic like Origen.[1] Finally amid this balance of
probabilities the Seventh General Council of the
Church (A.D. 787), in a case where history could
make no decision, used the voice of authority to
settle the question at issue and Eusebius stood
condemned as an Arian at last. But the matter cannot rest with such a condemnation. We must now
consider how Eusebius acted in these stormy years
that followed the Council of Nicaea, and see if any
elucidation of the question at issue can be attained.[2]

[1] Eusebius is a saint in an Arian martyrology of about
380 A.D. (*Acta Sanctorum, Novembris*, Tomi II Pars Prior,
Brussels, 1894, p. lvii). In *Act. Sanct., l.c.*, p. lxix the question
whether the martyrology is really Arian is discussed. The
entry 'Arius Alexandriae presbyter' need not refer to the
heretic, as Arius is a name of common occurrence.
[2] On the seventh canon of Nicaea, which refers to the sees
of Caesarea and Jerusalem, see *infra*, chap. VI, pp. 134–5.

CHAPTER VI

The Attack on the Catholic Leaders

The Council of Nicaea was not a pleasant subject for Eusebius. His *Church History*, which had been enlarged in successive editions to include each new triumph of the Church, stops short at a point where its continuance would have made it of the greatest value. At the very end of his life Eusebius wrote a glowing account of the Council in his *Life of Constantine*, a work in which, however, he had so circumscribed the scope of his narrative, that the story given there of the meeting of the Council is very different from an account given in a history. In view of the circumstances, one cannot wonder at the fact that the *Church History* concludes with the final victory of Constantine over Licinius. So far Eusebius had omitted all reference to the Arian controversy and, if he had written a history of his own times and his own part in Church affairs, he would have been further from obtaining that peace[1] at which he aimed; his work would have been attacked by either or both of the contending parties. Eusebius lay low and said nothing.

From Nicaea Eusebius brought back a certificate of rehabilitation, a new creed, and a new friend-

---

[1] Cf. Letter of Eusebius to the Caesarean Church.

ship with no less a person than the Emperor
himself. His admiration for Constantine was un-
bounded and in the Emperor reposed his chief
hope for peace.

Constantine did his best to allay the misgivings
of the bishops by the splendour of his entertainment
at the Vicennalia, which took place immediately
after the Council. Eusebius delivered[1] an oration,
but has preserved no details of its content except
that it was a panegyric of the victorious Emperor.
Even though the *Life of Constantine* is not sober
history, we can have no doubt that Eusebius
enjoyed the celebrations, which surpassed all description[2] and seemed a visible representation of
the Kingdom of Christ on earth—a representation
with which Cerinthus[3] and other heretics would
have concurred, had they lived in this fortunate
generation.

The echoes of the Vicennalia had hardly died
away when the spirit of strife and faction broke out
again, notwithstanding the express wish of Constantine[4] that all should live at peace, and a most
discreditable period of ecclesiastical history began.
Egypt[5] was the seat of war at the start. Eusebius

[1] *V.C.* I. 1, IV. 46.
[2] See *V.C.* III. 15, 16.
[3] See *H.E.* III. 28. 5.
[4] *V.C.* III. 21.
[5] *V.C.* III. 23.

refuses to give the cause, but from another source[1]
we find that the ὁμοούσιος was troubling some
people, and that from his silence on this point
Eusebius got the reputation in certain quarters of
having dissembled at Nicaea. But how could he
tell the exact cause? He disapproved of the strife,
but if he explained that the cause of the trouble
was the inability of a party in Egypt to accept the
ὁμοούσιος he would thereby be giving his approval
to a word which he hated, and which he never
defended. The hope of peace which had operated
so strongly in influencing the mind of Eusebius at
Nicaea was not to be realised; during the next ten
years he was in the forefront of the theological
struggle, years in which the 'Nicene' leaders discovered that the weapon of State interference was
a dangerous one to use in settling Church disputes
and that it recoiled with terrific force.

For the moment the ascendancy of the Nicene
party was complete; the two great Eastern sees,
Alexandria and Antioch, were filled by Alexander
and Eustathius, both strong supporters of the
Council; on Alexander's death in 328, the election
of Athanasius, a young cleric who was an uncompromising and brilliant opponent of the opinions
of Arius, still further strengthened their position.
But the ascendancy was transient and even at the

---

[1] Socrates, *H.E.* I. 23, ἡ τοῦ ὁμοουσίου λέξις τινὰς
διετάραττεν.

time of the election of Athanasius the Arian reaction had begun, and soon both Eustathius and Athanasius were ejected.

Eustathius was the first to suffer. He had been a leading member of the Nicene Council—Theodoret[1] calls Athanasius ὁ τοῦ Εὐσταθίου συναγωνιστής, though we must remember that Eustathius is one of Theodoret's heroes.[2] The Bishop of Antioch was under no illusions about the lack of conviction which had characterised the signing of the Nicene Creed in certain quarters, and the different interpretations to which it was subjected. He attacked Eusebius of Caesarea for perverting the Nicene faith,[3] a thing which he (Eusebius) certainly had done in his letter to his Church, and he assailed Paulinus of Tyre and Patrophilus of Scythopolis as well. Eusebius retorted that he held the Nicene faith, and carried the war into the enemy's country by accusing the Bishop of Antioch of Sabellianism. Sozomen[4] states that Eustathius was attacked because of his steadfast defence of the Nicene decisions; the rights and wrongs of the case cannot be discovered, as the documents of the actual controversy are lost, but Socrates and Sozomen are unable to comprehend why Eustathius and Eusebius could not agree. Rivalry between

---

[1] *H.E.* i. 8.   [2] *H.E.* i. 20.
[3] Socrates, *H.E.* i. 23. Sozomen, *H.E.* ii. 18.
[4] Sozomen, *H.E.* ii. 19.

109

their sees and opposed views about Origen[1] probably served to embitter the relations of the two
bishops. There seems little reason to accept the
view[2] that Eusebius of Caesarea was the 'prime
mover' of a conspiracy to get rid of Eustathius at
any cost. Eustathius attacked Eusebius first, and
Eusebius by replying to the doctrinal attack against
himself commenced[3] the agitation against the
Bishop of Antioch which culminated in his condemnation, but one can be content to leave the
invention of the grosser charges to the fertile
imagination of Eusebius of Nicomedia and the
pronounced Arians.

So narrow was the path of theological rectitude,
that Eustathius may quite well have lapsed, perhaps unwittingly, into Sabellian expressions.[4] But

[1] R. V. Sellers, *Eustathius of Antioch*, p. 32, note 3, gives
a list of the sarcastic and slighting expressions used by
Eustathius with regard to Origen.

[2] Given in *D.C.B.* vol. II, p. 382, art. 'Eustathius'.

[3] Sellers, *op. cit.* pp. 42–6, relying on the evidence of
Eus. *V.C.* III. 59–62, thinks that there was considerable strife
within the Church at Antioch itself, through the refusal of
Eustathius to accept certain candidates for ordination. This
view seems very likely.

[4] Cf. Sellers, *op. cit.* p. 47, 'Eustathius' teaching, with its
insistence on the unity of the Divinity, cannot be explained
satisfactorily unless we are prepared to see in it a doctrinal
basis akin to that of Sabellianism'. But cf. p. 86 also, 'one
may assume that Eusebius of Caesarea, in making such an
accusation (i.e. of Sabellianism), had been led away from

Eusebius of Nicomedia and Theognis of Nicaea, by chance or design, visited the East and willingly lent a hand in the attack on Eustathius, with the feeling that the sympathy of the court was with their cause. The charge of Sabellianism was not enough, and a scandalous life as well was imputed to Eustathius. Whether the story in Theodoret is true or not in substance, it seems probable that some such charge was brought, through the hints given by Socrates and Sozomen. Another account of the indictment, recorded by Athanasius,[1] is that Eustathius had shown disrespect to Helena, mother of Constantine—a charge which may be true when we remember the regard of Helena for the martyr Lucian of Antioch, whose doctrinal position was very different from that of Eustathius.

We do not know exactly what part Eusebius of Caesarea took in the good work, but he is not named as an accuser of Eustathius in the charge of heresy. Cyrus of Beroea, rightly or wrongly,[2] is given this position. But it seems certain that Eusebius was present—perhaps he lent an air of respectability to proceedings which were otherwise

the truth through his animosity against Eustathius'. It is a pity that the actual documents of the controversy have perished.

[1] *Hist. Arian. ad Monachos*, 5; cf. Duchesne, *Early History of the Church*, Eng. transl. vol. II, p. 129.

[2] Socrates, *H.E.* I. 24. A very doubtful point; Cyrus himself was later deposed on the same charge.

somewhat disreputable. Such a trial could have only one result—Eustathius was exiled and never regained his see; Constantine heard the condemned bishop's view of the proceedings from his own lips[1] but did not restore him.

It is likely that the case of Asclepas of Gaza came up for consideration at this time. This bishop obtained a rehabilitation from the Council of Sardica in 344 after having been ejected for seventeen years from his bishopric.[2] Thus the present Council in Antioch, which took place in 330 or 331, cannot have been the original hearing of his case. That it was subject to an enquiry at Antioch is proved by the letter of the Council of Sardica preserved by Athanasius.[3] At that Council Asclepas brought forward a document relating to an inquiry which took place at Antioch, in the presence of his accusers and of Eusebius of Caesarea, and at which his innocence was proved.[4] We must regard this as an appeal from the condemnation by some local Synod which had ejected Asclepas soon after Nicaea. He did not regain his position, notwithstanding this inquiry, for some reason unknown. We cannot tell the relation of Eusebius to him, whether he was accuser or judge or both. The

[1] Eus. *V.C.* III. 60.

[2] Hilary, Frag. *Hist.* II. 6, III. 11 (Migne, *P.L.* vol. x, cols. 636, 666).

[3] Athanasius, *Apol. c. Arianos*, 47.   [4] Socrates, II. 23.

second alternative seems most likely as Eusebius is named apart from the accusers.

The ejection of Eustathius, like the ejection of Paul sixty years before, produced a formidable schism in the Church at Antioch. The bishop had a large following, and the city was so stirred that bloodshed almost ensued. Matters were complicated by the fact that the successor of Eustathius, Paulinus[1] of Tyre, died after six months in office, and so an opportunity was provided for the breaking forth again of passions which time might have allayed. The selection of Paulinus, an opponent of Eustathius, shows the biased nature of the Council, but we must remember that Paulinus had been a presbyter[2] of the Church of Antioch, and would have many friends there. The fact of his episcopate we cannot doubt; Eusebius, his friend, states it as a fact in the *Contra Marcellum*,[3] and this is the only point in time at which it can be placed: it is very hard to imagine an Arian Paulinus coming between an orthodox Philogonius and an orthodox Eustathius, i.e. in A.D. 324. The words (πάλαι κεκοιμη-μένος) which Eusebius uses of his friend could quite well refer to the five years or so between the

[1] Philostorgius, *H.E.* IV. 7, 15.
[2] Eus. *C.M.* I. 4. 2.
[3] *C.M. loc. cit.* On the whole question of Paulinus see an article by G. Bardy in *Revue des Sciences religieuses*, vol. II, 1922, pp. 35 ff.

death of Paulinus and the writing of the work against Marcellus.

Eulalius, the next bishop, died almost immediately after his election, and there were considerable troubles in the city. Constantine had already taken a hand in the matter, and had addressed letters[1] on the subject to the Antiochenes, which Eusebius forebore to include in the *Life of Constantine* because they might damage the reputation of the accused, and renew the memory of evils. This statement seems to show that Eusebius' anger against Eustathius did not last for ever.

The next person to be elected Bishop of Antioch was Eusebius of Caesarea. The people were enthusiastic in their approval,[2] but the Eustathians had probably by this time withdrawn from the deliberations. Eusebius wisely refused the honour, for which he would have been unsuited. His place was the library of Caesarea, not the 'inferno'[3] at Antioch. Eusebius based his refusal on the fifteenth canon of Nicaea, which forbade the translation of a bishop from one see to another. The rule had already been broken by the election of Paulinus, but it had been broken for an Arian by Arians, who felt no scruples about such an act. Eusebius was not an Arian, and, moreover, it would have ill

[1] Eus. *V.C.* III. 59.
[2] Eus. *V.C.* III. 60. 3 (Letter of Constantine).
[3] Duchesne, *op. cit.* Eng. transl. vol. II, p. 131.

become one who had recently rebutted an accusation of having perverted the Nicene faith to show so little respect for another decision of the Council of Nicaea. The choice of Eusebius as Bishop of Antioch was a very natural one. He was in high favour with the Emperor, and his moderate position might well lead to a healing of the Antiochene troubles. Moreover, the Arians knew that he would be harmless, and would not interfere with their future machinations.

Eusebius, as has been already noted, did not include in the *Life of Constantine* any letters of the Emperor which might react to the damage of the reputation of anyone concerned. He inserted three,[1] written with the aim of restoring unity and peace, and all three relate to his own refusal, in which Constantine fully concurred. The first of these is to the people of Antioch, the second to Eusebius himself, and the third to the assembled bishops. The moment was really the greatest one in Eusebius' life, and the letters must have been an abiding satisfaction to him. In the letters Constantine praised the learning and virtue of the Bishop of Caesarea,[2] and declared that Eusebius was, in the judgement of the world, fit to be bishop of any church.[3] The Emperor suggested to the

[1] *V.C.* III. 60–2.
[2] *V.C.* III. 60. 3.
[3] *V.C.* III. 61. 1, πάσης ἐκκλησίας or 'of the whole church'?.

assembled bishops two candidates,[1] one of whom, Euphronius, was chosen, but he also soon died, and Flacillus became bishop and succeeded in surviving for about nine years in an office that had proved so fatal to his immediate predecessors. The Arians had gained their first great victory; it was but a stepping-stone to the next.

Eustathius had been deposed in A.D. 330 or 331. By this time various machinations were in progress against Athanasius, but, up to the time of the deposition of the Bishop of Antioch, he had managed to retain his see and the esteem of the Emperor, though attacked within Egypt by faction, which was encouraged by the Arians from without. Athanasius proved himself very unyielding: to us he may appear obstinately unyielding, but it is hard to see how he could have acted in any other way. The chief point on which he came to grief was his refusal to re-admit Arius to the Church, notwithstanding the fact that the Emperor regarded the heretic as having presented a creed sufficiently orthodox as to justify his return. In this matter Athanasius was in a hopeless position; if he received Arius the machinations of his enemies would be strengthened in Egypt—a genuine reconciliation was hardly possible; if he rejected Arius he was bound to suffer the imperial displeasure, for Constantine was falling more and

[1] *V.C.* III. 62. 2.

more under the influence of Arians, who knew[1] that they could not triumph so long as Athanasius held his position, and who persuaded Constantine to order[2] Athanasius to receive into the Church all who desired communion. A doctrinal attack on the Bishop of Alexandria was an impossibility, and he was made the subject of various charges which may appear to us absurd and malicious, but to which he had probably contributed to a great extent by the obstinacy of his resistance and a certain want of tact. In the attack on Athanasius, Eusebius of Caesarea played a prominent part, though Athanasius shows no resentment towards him, as he does towards his namesake of Nicomedia.

Of all the charges brought against Athanasius the most absurd, and yet the most deadly, was that he had killed a Meletian bishop named Arsenius after having cut off his hand for the purpose of magic. Moreover, his position was rendered worse by the fact that Constantine with singular injustice —whatever might be his personal opinion of Athanasius—allowed an old charge,[3] which he had dismissed as void of foundation when the accused visited him in the end of 331 or beginning of 332, to be raked up again. A Synod was summoned to

[1] Socrates, *H.E.* I. 23.
[2] Athanasius, *Apol. c. Arianos*, 8. Sozomen, *H.E.* II. 22.
[3] The affair of the chalice of Ischyras.

117

meet at Caesarea in the spring[1] of 334 to consider the question of Arsenius in particular, and we may presume the other charges, including violence to opponents[2] in general, but Athanasius, knowing that he would receive no mercy, refused to attend, and the Synod, after waiting in vain, broke up.[3] Sozomen[4] says that he refused because he feared the deceit of Eusebius of Caesarea, Eusebius of Nicomedia, and their friends, while Theodoret[5] states that Constantine changed the place of meeting from Caesarea to Tyre since he suspected that Athanasius would not attend at Caesarea, because of the bishop of that place. So far we have no evidence of open hostility between Athanasius and Eusebius of Caesarea, but various causes must have contributed to create ill-feeling between them. Eusebius had, rightly or wrongly, taken part, and a prominent part, in the deposition of Eustathius; his greatest friends were Arians; his reverence for Constantine would intensify his objection to Athanasius, who set himself against the Emperor.

The postponed Council met at Tyre in 335, and the Arians made sure of Athanasius' attendance by the issue of an imperial command[6] threatening any-

---

[1] H. Idris Bell, *Jews and Christians in Egypt*, p. 48.
[2] Cf. Sozomen, *loc. cit.*; Bell, *op. cit.* 47. These charges of violence were true to some extent at any rate.
[3] Sozomen, *H.E.* II. 25.   [4] *H.E.* II. 25.
[5] *H.E.* I. 26.   [6] Eus. *V.C.* IV. 42.

one who failed to attend, when summoned, with exile. This was a direct hit at Athanasius. He attended with many of his Egyptian supporters. Never had any writer of tragedy[1] or comedy produced a plot like those which the Arians manufactured against him. The proceedings were indeed farcical, if they had not had such serious results. And yet Eusebius of Caesarea, with others, was judge, appointed by the Emperor himself.[2] It will be seen at once that there is some conflict between the evidence of Epiphanius and that of Theodoret, who stresses the fact that Constantine changed the place of meeting to Tyre because of the antipathy of Athanasius to our Eusebius. Now it is unlikely that Constantine would do such a thing and then appoint Eusebius one of the judges. It seems preferable to accept Epiphanius; Athanasius had as much reason to refuse to attend at Tyre as at Caesarea, because he must have known that the trial would have the same result, irrespective of place.

The accounts of the Council of Tyre are somewhat unsatisfactory, but all are agreed on the disorderly character of the proceedings, during which accusations and taunts were flung recklessly. The accusation of Eusebius of Caesarea by Potam-

[1] Theodoret, *H.E.* I. 26.
[2] Epiphanius, *Haer.* LXVIII. 8. Philostorgius, *H.E.* II. 11 (p. 23, ll. 11 ff., Bidez).

mon has already[1] been mentioned. Rufinus[2] and
Sozomen make the principals, in a somewhat
similar story, Paphnutius and Maximus, Bishop of
Jerusalem. But the Epiphanius version gets some
confirmation from a letter of the Catholic Egyptian
bishops in support of Athanasius[3] and therefore
seems the more likely of the two. As usual on these
occasions, a woman of ill repute was produced
against the accused, who vindicated his character
triumphantly. Philostorgius,[4] the Arian historian,
puts the case the opposite way and makes Athanasius produce the woman against Eusebius. But this
looks like an Arian invention in order to blacken
the character of Athanasius still more.

Eusebius then endured the taunt of Potammon:
he saw Arsenius produced alive with two hands and
persuaded of his own identity: he heard the cry of
'Magic', with which this sight was hailed.[5] By the
intervention of Dionysius, the imperial commissioner who had the unenviable task of keeping the
shepherds of the flock of Christ in order, Athanasius
was saved from actual violence. What was the
attitude of Eusebius of Caesarea?

A commission had been sent by the Council to

[1] *Supra*, chap. III, pp. 51–2.
[2] Rufinus, *H.E.* x. 19 (p. 993, ll. 18 ff., Mommsen).
Sozomen, *H.E.* II. 25.
[3] Athanasius, *Apol. c. Arianos*, 8.
[4] Philostorgius, *H.E.* II. 11 (p. 23, l. 15, Bidez).
[5] Theodoret, I. 30.

the Mareotis in Egypt to investigate a charge of
violence against one Ischyras, the head of the
Meletian Church there, and the members of this
commission were all violent enemies of Athanasius.
The Egyptian bishops at Tyre wrote various letters
to the assembled bishops and to Dionysius, pro-
testing against this partisan inquiry. Now in these
letters Eusebius of Caesarea is not one of the 'gang'
which was out to ruin Athanasius; the members of
this body were Eusebius of Nicomedia, Theognis
of Nicaea, Maris of Chalcedon, Narcissus of Neronias, Theodorus of Heraclea, and Patrophilus of
Scythopolis, and also, according to one letter,
Flacillus of Antioch. At any rate these are the
names given by the supporters of Athanasius, who
would not, presumably, have omitted Eusebius of
Caesarea had he been one of their violent opponents. They mention him only once, and then in a
curiously cryptic way. The letter to all the bishops
closes with the words, 'for you indeed know that they
(i.e. the above-mentioned list) are our enemies, and
owing to what cause Eusebius of Caesarea has
become our enemy since last year'.[1] Something
had happened to widen the gulf between Eusebius
and the Athanasians, and that something had
happened within a quite short space of time before
the holding of the Council of Tyre. Had the
abortive Council of Caesarea anything to do with

[1] Athanasius, *Apol. c. Arianos*, 77.

it? Was Eusebius angry at the suspicion with which Athanasius regarded him, and with his refusal to appear for judgement at Caesarea? Or had he been irritated by the whole Athanasian policy of uncompromising hostility to the erstwhile presbyter of Alexandria and his friends who now rejoiced in an imperial rehabilitation? Who was this troublesome Athanasius anyhow? He had been a mere deacon at Nicaea. What right had he to cause all this stir and confusion in the Church? How arrogant these Egyptians were! We here must call to mind the reply of Eusebius to the taunt of Potammon:[1] 'If you come hither and make such accusations against us, then do your accusers speak the truth. For if you tyrannise here, much more do you in your own country'.

We can hardly imagine that Eusebius was so deeply involved in his researches at Caesarea as to be a complete dupe of the Arian party, and that he really believed all the charges brought against Athanasius to be true. If past experience of controversy availed him nothing, the actual trial of Athanasius must have openly shown the absurdity of the whole thing. But as we have seen, he realised how uncompromising the Egyptian clergy were, and how hard it was to decide which side was the worse. Recent investigations show that the Atha-

[1] Epiphanius, *Haer.* LXVIII. 8 (Migne, *P.G. Epiphanius*, vol. II, col. 197), as translated by McGiffert, *op. cit.* p. 9.

nasians were every whit as bad as their opponents.[1]
But Eusebius was not much good in dealing with
men; he was at the mercy of the stronger party.
At Nicaea he swallowed creed and anathemas; at
Tyre he allowed his Arian friends to use him for
their own purposes, to lend an air of respectability
to their malice: but all the while he was not an
Arian.

Athanasius fled to the Emperor, and was, of
course, condemned in his absence. He was deposed
and forbidden to return to Alexandria. The condemnation was based[2] on his refusal to appear at
Caesarea, where the bishops had waited in vain
for him, on the fact that he brought so many
supporters to Tyre as to create disturbances, on his
declining to reply to accusations against him, on his
attacks on the honour of certain bishops, and on
his sometimes not obeying when summoned by the
bishops, and at other times not deigning to be
judged. Finally, the commissioners from Egypt
reported that the chalice of Ischyras had been
broken.

In Tyre Eusebius was a very unheroic figure,
but when the Council adjourned to Jerusalem[3] for
the dedication of the new church there—which took
place in the year of the Tricennalia of Constantine,
just as the Council of Nicaea had met in the year

[1] Bell, *op. cit.* pp. 53 ff.
[2] Sozomen, *H.E.* ii. 25.   [3] See Eus. *V.C.* iv. 43-5.

of the twentieth anniversary of his accession—he found his best form and delivered not one but several orations. Arius and his friends were re-admitted to the Church, and the celebrations passed off merrily, though their close was over-shadowed by a not too attractive summons from the Emperor who desired the presence of the bishops to consider the case of Athanasius in Con-stantinople itself.[1] The bishops rushed home to escape the summons,[2] but supporters of Athanasius were deterred from going to his assistance by the guile of the Arians[3] who concealed the true import of the Emperor's letter. It is a remarkable fact that of the six bishops who attended four had to go in the direction of Constantinople to reach their sees: these four are Eusebius of Nicomedia, Theognis of Nicaea, Ursacius of Singidunum, and Valens of Mursa: the other two are Patrophilus of Scytho-polis and Eusebius of Caesarea. Of these two the former had been in the forefront of the Arian battalions from the earliest days of the controversy, and was apparently determined to pursue Atha-nasius to the bitter end; his episcopal neighbour, Eusebius, probably had to put in an appearance since he had presided at the Council of Tyre and, moreover, he was to preach the sermon at the Tricennalia. It seems likely that he had received

[1] Athanasius, *Apol. c. Arianos*, 86.
[2] Socrates, *H.E.* i. 35.　[3] Athanasius, *Apol. c. Arianos*, 87.

the invitation before matters had come to the present crisis.

The deputation seems to have had little difficulty in convincing Constantine that Athanasius was in the wrong. The Emperor was in no mood for lengthy discussion—but he saw that, innocent or guilty, Athanasius was an enemy to the peace of the Church at the moment. So Athanasius was sent to Gaul. The ancient authors, relying on the word of the accused himself,[1] though Sozomen dissents, state that the old charges were dropped—nothing more was said of them—and a new charge substituted, that Athanasius was determined to cut off the corn supply from Constantinople. He was banished at once, notwithstanding his protests. The celebration of the Tricennalia was to proceed unclouded by the thought of renewal of this interminable quarrel. But we may note that no successor was appointed to Athanasius: his was not to be a life sentence.

Having now got rid of their chief opponent, the Arians pursued a lesser, but by no means despicable, adversary, Marcellus of Ancyra, who had been a leading supporter of the 'orthodox' party at the Council of Nicaea,[2] and had, at the time when he was attacked, been a bishop[3] for many years. He

[1] Athanasius, *Apol. c. Arianos*, 9, 87.
[2] Athanasius, *Apol. c. Arianos*, 23, 32.
[3] Eusebius, *C.M.* ii. 1. 9. *E.Th.* ii. 22. 4.

had assailed the Arians in a book: Asterius a sophist, Eusebius the Great, i.e. of Nicomedia, Paulinus of Tyre, Origen, Narcissus of Neronias, and finally 'the other Eusebius' (i.e. of Caesarea), were all named and attacked. If this had been the sum of his misdeeds Marcellus might have escaped, but he had offended the 'gang' by his refusal to concur in the decisions of the Council of Tyre, and to take part in the Jerusalem celebrations,[1] a circumstance which could quite easily be construed into disrespect for the Emperor. He was therefore condemned by a Synod of Constantinople[2] (A.D. 336) after his case had been discussed at Jerusalem in the previous year.

The persons attacked by Marcellus have already been named and Eusebius of Caesarea found himself openly shown up as one of the company with whom he had associated for so long. The Synod showed considerable astuteness in licensing the Bishop of Caesarea to conduct the refutation of Marcellus: besides being the most competent theo-

[1] Sozomen, *H.E.* II. 33. Socrates, *H.E.* I. 36, also deals with the case of Marcellus.

[2] The Synod which condemned him was composed of bishops from Pontus, Cappadocia, Asia, Phrygia, Bithynia, Thrace, and the parts beyond (Eus. *C.M.* II. 4. 29 (58. 8)), i.e. there is no mention of the presence of Eastern bishops. We have already seen that only Eusebius and Patrophilus had obeyed the Emperor's summons to consider the case of Athanasius.

logian, Eusebius was not an Arian: the doctrinal cause of the attack on Marcellus was his lapse, presumably from Nicene orthodoxy, into Sabellianism, and it would have been too blatant a misdemeanour even for Arians, if one of themselves, who had quite ostensibly never even approximated to belief in the Nicene Creed, had written attacking one who had violated it.

The works which Eusebius wrote against Marcellus, the *Contra Marcellum* and the *De Ecclesiastica Theologia*, are much more in conformity with orthodoxy than any of his earlier ones.[1] And yet in the *Contra Marcellum*, at any rate, Eusebius had to defend the character of his Arian friends as well as his own. He writes from a detached point of view, referring to himself as ἕτερος Εὐσέβιος, and puts himself on the same footing as the rest of Marcellus' enemies. He conducts the defence of his friends very badly; he adopts his usual method of letting his subject speak for himself, and the work consists largely in extracts from Marcellus, with comments by Eusebius. He does not specifically defend the views of those who were attacked with him but merely says—'they are well known; their character is proof against such assaults, while the blasphemy of Marcellus against Christ is not doubtful or unknown'.[2] Marcellus has proved himself a bad shepherd, because, instead of at-

[1] Cf. Socrates, *H.E.* II. 21.   [2] *C.M.* I. I. 6.

tacking the heretics in his own diocese, he has chosen to attack the ministers of God. Eusebius then proceeds[1] to show how Marcellus misused and altered the Scriptures: he shows very little charity to his opponent who was, we may be sure, quoting the correct Ancyrean text, and the refutation by Eusebius would therefore be worse than useless so far as the supporters of Marcellus in his own diocese were concerned—yet Eusebius was a leading authority on texts, and ought to have known how the copies of the Scriptures varied in different Churches.

In actual matters connected with the Bible, Eusebius gets the better of Marcellus at several points: though the points are small, they represent tactical successes for Eusebius: if Marcellus does not know the Bible, how can he be a good guide in spiritual things? To inaccurate quotation from the Bible Marcellus joined a knowledge of Greek proverbs.[2] He compares these with the proverbs of Solomon and states that the same principle applies to both kinds, i.e. a proverb is a saying of which the sense is not apparent at the first glance. But Eusebius saw the difference between Greek and Hebrew proverbs. The Greek ones, on Marcellus' own showing, had their foundation in some event, those of Solomon cannot be interpreted εἰ μὴ κατὰ μόνην μεταφορὰν καὶ ἀναστροφὴν τῆς λέξεως.[3] They had no foundation in historical fact.

[1] C.M. I. 2.   [2] C.M. I. 3.   [3] C.M. I. 3. 16.

Eusebius next turns[1] to the attack made by Marcellus on the leaders of the Church whose names have already been given. He describes them as those who had written 'correctly and in harmony with the faith of the Church' (ὀρθῶς καὶ ἐκκλησιαστικῶς).[2] Asterius is not qualified by praise or blame; Eusebius of Nicomedia is 'the Great'—a term used to distinguish him from our Eusebius—whose episcopate many illustrious cities and provinces have desired.[3] Paulinus, as usual, receives the greatest praise. Narcissus is mentioned in a non-committal fashion. Origen stands in a different relation to the other persons attacked because he had been dead for a very long time (προπάλαι).[4] For us the most interesting fragments of Marcellus are those which Eusebius quotes against himself. The chief fault which Marcellus had to find with Eusebius was that he divided the Godhead and made the Logos ἕτερον Θεόν, οὐσίᾳ τε καὶ δυνάμει διεστῶτα τοῦ Πατρός,[5] and wrote that the image is not the same as that of which it is the image. Eusebius, as we have seen, regarded the Logos as Θεός. He recognises that the Son has a different οὐσία from the Father,[6] but this is merely a method of emphasising the distinct existence of the two persons. Eusebius had no doubts

---

[1] C.M. i. 4.   [2] C.M. i. 4. i.   [3] C.M. i. 4. 9.
[4] C.M. i. 4. 3.   [5] C.M. i. 4. 39 ff.
[6] P.E. vii. 15 (325 b); cf. D.E. iv. 3 (149 b); supra, p. 84.

whatever about the 'generatio ex substantia Patris'.
Marcellus makes much of this point. His sources
are, as given by Eusebius: (1) a letter[1] written by
Narcissus of Neronias, in which Hosius is represented as asking the writer if like Eusebius of
Palestine he believed in 'two essences'; (2) some
writing of Eusebius himself which is not preserved[2]
but which is probably the same as the letter mentioned by Eusebius later;[3] (3) reports of what
Eusebius said, preaching at Laodicea[4] and at
Ancyra.[5] Marcellus had not heard either sermon,
and Eusebius avers on the Ancyra one that he said
nothing more than St Paul in his Epistle to the
Galatians:[6] τέκνα μου, οὓς πάλιν ὠδίνω ἄχρις οὗ
μορφωθῇ Χριστὸς ἐν ὑμῖν. To this saying of St Paul
Marcellus sarcastically adds that Eusebius tra-
vailed a truly bitter and grievous travail, in that
he discovered that with regard to religion the
Galatians did not have the same views as himself, and say that there were two essences, two
elements, two powers, and two Gods.[7] But
Marcellus ruined his position, which was quite
tenable, by proceeding to declare that, according
to Eusebius, Christ was a 'mere man'.[8] He could
not have it both ways. Eusebius[9] again protests

[1] *C.M.* I. 4. 39. [2] *C.M.* I. 4. 40.
[3] *C.M.* I. 4. 65. [4] *C.M.* I. 4. 42.
[5] *C.M.* I. 4. 45. [6] iv. 19. [7] *C.M.* I. 4. 45.
[8] *C.M.* I. 4. 46, 55 ff. [9] *C.M.* I. 4. 65.

that he was only quoting St Paul[1] and declares that Marcellus slandered the apostle. In connection with this point Marcellus reveals an interesting glimpse of the character of Eusebius:[2] 'he prided himself excessively on his power of remembering the Scriptures'. Another point on which Marcellus took Eusebius to task was the statement[3] that there was only one true God, i.e. the Father, from which Paulinus deduced that there were 'younger gods'. Eusebius retorts that Marcellus does not understand that the words used are not his own, but those of Christ Himself.[4] But looked at in a certain way, the statement of Paulinus might quite well be a development of the position of Eusebius. At the close of Book I Eusebius points out that the attack of Marcellus on himself relates to an infinitesimal portion of his works, only to part of a certain letter,[5] and that no attack was made on his works on the Scriptures, 'which are indeed in circulation everywhere': thus he pays a compliment to his own writings, or at any rate to the efficiency of the Caesarean copyists.

Book II deals with the opinions of Marcellus, who held doctrines akin to Sabellianism, if he did not actually hold to that heresy. Marcellus was fully aware that the stand which he took would be construed as Sabellianism by his adversaries and

[1] 1 Tim. ii. 5.   [2] *C.M.* I. 4. 60.   [3] *C.M.* I. 4. 50.
[4] St John xvii. 3.   [5] *C.M.* I. 4. 65.

he attacked Sabellius in his work in order to safeguard himself.[1] But the analogy, if not the coinci-
dence, between the two was so striking that his
plan could not save him. It is a mistake to suppose
that Eusebius did not recognise this point and that
'the adversaries of Marcellus, and in particular
Eusebius of Caesarea, pretend that his doctrine
has analogies with Sabellianism'.[2] Eusebius does
recognise some difference between Marcellus and
Sabellius: Marcellus did not use the words of
Sabellius in introducing God as a Son-Father, but
he introduces Him as such in actual fact.[3] This,
indeed, makes Marcellus far worse than Sabellius,
because Sabellius sinned unwittingly, whereas Marcellus sinned consciously.

The work *Against Marcellus* was regarded at first
by Eusebius as a sufficient refutation; he airily
dismisses his opponent by saying that the mere
exposition of the doctrines of Marcellus was enough.
But very soon he changed his mind and wrote the
three books *De Ecclesiastica Theologia*, lest the work
of Marcellus should seduce any from the true[4]
faith. He dedicated this work to Flacillus, Bishop
of Antioch. The dedicatory letter to Flacillus lays
special stress on the belief of Flacillus and Eusebius
in the Holy Trinity as opposed to the failure of

---

[1] See *E. Th.* I. 1, I. 19.
[2] Hefele, Fr. transl. 1907, vol. I. 2, p. 673.
[3] *E. Th.* I. 1. 2.   [4] *E. Th.* I. Preface, 2.

Marcellus to grant a separate existence to the Son.

In the *De Ecclesiastica Theologia* Eusebius makes no effort to defend the Nicene Creed specifically: he never mentions the great Council and the word ὁμοούσιος is completely absent from his work. But he is very anxious to make it quite clear that he is proclaiming what the Church teaches; there is now no question of his defending Arians, but he is making an assault on a heresy which he dreaded, and on opinions which he regarded as more pernicious than any that Arians had ever held. But he is very insistent in his condemnation of the Arian doctrine that the Son was produced ἐξ οὐκ ὄντων[1] and in his rejection of the word κτίσμα[2] as describing the relation of the Son to the Father. κτίσμα signifies something created, but not sharing the nature of the creator.

In this work Eusebius is also very explicit in showing that there is one God,[3] not two, a point with regard to which Marcellus had taken him to task. There is only one God since the Son recognises the Father as greater than Himself and

[1] *E.Th.* I. 9. 1, I. 10. 4, III. 2. 8.
[2] *E.Th.* I. 10. 4, III. 2. 8 ff., etc. Eusebius had, it must be admitted, gone the length of calling the Son κτίσμα τέλειον, in his letter to Alexander on behalf of Arius, who himself used this expression (Arius *ap.* Athanasius, *De Synodis*, 16).
[3] *E.Th.* II. 7 and II. 23.

133

worships[1] Him, because Father and Son do not
have the same honour—there is only one God,
the Father, notwithstanding the two ὑποστάσεις.[2]
Eusebius retracts somewhat also from a former
position, by allowing to the Son the title ἀληθινὸς
θεός, ἐν εἰκόνι, i.e. as the Son is the perfect image
of the Father so He bears the Father's titles 'in
image' also.[3] Eusebius regarded his work as very
short (ἐν ἐπιτόμῳ);[4] though it extends to three
books, it is short compared with the works of his
earlier days.

Marcellus' work was pronounced orthodox by
the Council of Sardica, which, being a Western
Council, only understood the questions at issue in
the East indifferently.[5] It was alleged in his defence
that statements put forward by him tentatively had
been construed by his opponents into dogmatic
pronouncements. But Marcellus had probably
altered his book in the intervening time in order
to secure a reversal of judgement.

With the writing of these two works the part of
Eusebius in the Arian controversy was concluded,
but before leaving it mention must be made of a
passage in Sozomen,[6] which refers to Macarius,

[1] E. Th. II. 7. 1, 12.
[2] E. Th. II. 7. 1.
[3] E. Th. II. 23. 2.
[4] Letter to Flacillus.
[5] Harnack, Hist. Dog. Eng. transl. vol. IV, p. 66, note.
[6] H.E. II. 20.

134

the orthodox Bishop of Jerusalem. As Metropolitan of Palestine, Eusebius had had his supremacy confirmed by the seventh canon of Nicaea, which, nevertheless, gave special honour to the Bishop of Jerusalem, after the Bishop of Caesarea. But it is plain that the campaign of aggrandisement of the Jerusalem Church was already proceeding; and the seventh canon attempted to strike a mean by giving a certain precedence to Jerusalem, as a unique Church, while keeping it in subjection to its metropolitan. The passage of Sozomen in question refers to the election of Maximus, who was kept by Macarius as his prospective successor, because he (Macarius) was afraid that Eusebius and Patrophilus and their friends would elect an Arian to such an important position. The historian states that Macarius excommunicated them (apparently including Eusebius, his metropolitan), when they attempted innovations in his lifetime. This excommunication of a metropolitan by one of his suffragans casts doubt on the authenticity of the narrative, and, in any case, an indefinite φασί is Sozomen's sole authority; the story of the resistance of Macarius to his superior could well be an invention of the time at which Sozomen wrote, an invention designed to aid the Jerusalem Church towards the consummation reached in 451 at the Council of Chalcedon.

The Seventh General Synod saw in Eusebius a

double-minded man, unstable in all his ways.[1]
All his writings and epistles went to show how far
his heart was from the truth. Yet Eusebius states
in his refutation of Marcellus that his opponent
could only find part of a certain letter among his
works, on which to base his attack. As we have
seen, Eusebius did not by any means go the whole
way with the Arians in his works, but he was with
them in all their acts after the Council of Nicaea.
In the cases of Eustathius and Marcellus he did not
begin the strife: in the case of Athanasius he
probably realised that one side was quite as bad
as the other. These circumstances conspired to make
him the tool of his friends. He really belonged to
the third century, not to the fourth; his interest lay
in ἀρχαῖα.[2] At Nicaea he was carried away by his
desire for peace and by the influence of the Emperor, after Nicaea he was carried away by his
friends. Unfitted by training, and apparently by
nature, to control men, he was unable to influence
those who traded upon his reputation in order to
carry out their own doubtful transactions.

[1] Migne, *P.L.* vol. cxxix, col. 428.
[2] Leclercq, *op. cit.* col. 766, 'ce mot ἀρχαῖα, qui porte avec
lui comme une séduction de sincérité'.

INDEX

I GENERAL

137

INDEX

Clarus of Ptolemais, 12
Claudius, 8
Clement of Alexandria, 31 n., 44
Clementine Homilies, 5
Clementine Recognitions, 6
Cleopatra (1), 1 n.
Cleopatra (2), 2
Constantine, 30, 42, 43, 91–9,
103, 106, 107, 111, 114–19,
123–5
Constantinople, 124–6
Conybeare, 71 n.
Corduba, 92
Cornelius, 12, 13
Cowper, 93 n.
Cureton, 24 n., 49 n., 55 n.,
56 n., 60 n.
Cyril of Antioch, 29
Cyrus of Beroea, 111
Cyzicus, 105

D'Alès, 77 n.
Daniel, 38 n.
De Boor, 26 n.
Decian Persecution, 16
Demetrius of Alexandria, 14, 89
Diocletian, 30, 46
Diodorus of Tarsus, 41
Dionysius (Imperial Commissioner), 120, 121
Dionysius of Alexandria, 19,
26, 29 n., 78, 86
Dionysius of Rome, 19, 20, 86
Dionysus, 11
Domnus, 17
Donatists, 73, 94 n.
Dora, 1, 2
Dorotheus, 29, 50
Drusus, 5
Duchesne, 105 n., 111 n.,
114 n.

Edom, 11

Egypt, 3, 70–2, 107, 108, 116,
121, 123
Eli, 44
Emmaus, 39
Epiphanius, 6, 105, 119, 120
Eulalius, 114
Euphronius, 116
Eusebius of Alexandria, 28
Eusebius of Caesarea, 5 n., 10,
17; life, etc.:
life of, by Acacius, 18
date of birth of, 18–20
Christian born or convert,
20–2
relations of, with Pamphilus,
22 ff.
textual work of, 24, 33
ignorance of Roman History
of, 26, 38
friends of, 27–9, 59–60, 113,
126–7, 136
on the Roman Empire, 29–
30, 46–7
relations of, with Constantine,
30, 103, 107
on the Jews, 31–2
scope of works of, 33–4
suspected forgery by, 34–5
method of work of, 35–6
on persecution, 45–7
movements of, in the great
persecution, 49–51, 55–6
arrested, 51–4
at Council of Tyre, 51–2,
119–23
on John the Egyptian, 55
reports miracles, 61–2
supports Arius, 74–5
confusion in the mind of, 77
doctrinal relation of, to Origen, 78–85
doctrinal relation of, to Dionysius and Theognostus, 86–8

139

INDEX

II GREEK

Only important words are included in this Index.